Harriet Tubman,

SECRET

AGENT

HOW DARING SLAVES AND FREE BLACKS SPIED FOR THE UNION DURING THE CIVIL WAR

THOMAS B. ALLEN

Featuring illustrations by Carla Bauer

NATIONAL GEOGRAPHIC
Washington, D.C.

For my grandchildren, with all my love for them.

Text copyright © 2006 Thomas B. Allen.
Illustrations copyright © 2006 Carla Bauer.

ACKNOWLEDGMENTS: Without the help I received at libraries and archives, this book would not have been written. My research took me to the Library of Congress, the National Archives, and The American University, along with public libraries in Maryland, Virginia, North Carolina, and South Carolina. I was given much help at every place, but I wish especially to thank Marianne Cawley, of the Charleston (South Carolina) Public Library and staff members of the Museum of the Confederacy in Richmond, Virginia.

And at my side, searching through folders and microfilms, was my wife, Scottie. Thanks, too, to others who helped, including Kate Clifford Larson, Hayden B. Peake, Barbara Mackey, Cynthia H. Porcher, Vicki Sandstead, and four members of the sharp-eyed Warner family: Dorothy, Michael, Charlie, and Annie, who read this book before it became a book. Special appreciation goes to Carla Bauer, whose woodcuts capture the flavor of the period.

I am once more in debt to Suzanne, Nancy, Bea, David, Lori, Susan, Ruthie, Carl, Steve, and the rest of the terrific staff at National Geographic Children's Books.

Book design by Bea Jackson and David M. Seager. Production design by Ruthie Thompson. Text is set in Caslon Antique.

HALF TITLE PAGE: Beneath the flags of the Union and Confederacy is a symbol of slavery: a copper badge that identified a slave who could be hired out by his or her owner.
TITLE PAGE: Fighting for the Union in the Civil War, Harriet Tubman becomes a spy in Confederate territory.

Scholastic Book Club edition ISBN-10: 1-4263-0110-3; ISBN-13: 978-1-4263-0110-0

Library of Congress Cataloging-in-Publication Data
Allen, Thomas B.
Harriet Tubman, secret agent : how daring slaves and free Blacks spied for the Union
during the Civil War / written by Thomas B. Allen ; with illustrations by Carla Bauer.
p. cm.
Includes bibliographical references and index.
ISBN-10: 0-7922-7889-5 (hardcover); 0-7922-7890-9 (library binding)
ISBN-13: 978-0-7922-7889-4 (hardcover); 978-0-7922-7890-0 (library binding)
1. Tubman, Harriet, 1820?–1913 — Juvenile literature. 2. Slaves — United States —
Biography — Juvenile literature. 3. African American women — Biography — Juvenile
literature. 4. Underground railroad — Juvenile literature. I. Bauer, Carla, ill. II. Title.
E444.T82A73 2006   973.7'115–dc22   2005030927

Printed in the United States of America

Table of Contents.

	Cast of Key Characters.	6
Prologue.	Black Moses.	9
Chapter 1.	Harriet's Escape.	17
Chapter 2.	The Underground Railroad.	27
Chapter 3.	Slave Revolts.	37
Chapter 4.	John Brown Meets the General.	45
Chapter 5.	Trouble at Harpers Ferry.	57
Chapter 6.	The "Old Colored Woman."	67
Chapter 7.	Trouble in the Capital.	77
Chapter 8.	The Secret War.	83
Chapter 9.	Black Dispatches.	95
Chapter 10.	Black Spies and the Anaconda Plan.	113
Chapter 11.	Harriet Goes to War.	127
Chapter 12.	The General Leads a Raid.	139
Epilogue.	Telling the Secrets.	163
	Map and Time Line.	168
	Elizabeth Van Lew's Code.	172
	Text Notes.	173
	Quote Sources.	182
	Further Reading.	187
	Index.	189

❦ CAST OF KEY CHARACTERS ❦

(in order of appearance).

HARRIET TUBMAN
Born a slave in Maryland,
she escapes and becomes
the most famous
conductor on the
Underground Railroad
and a secret agent
in the Civil War.

FREDERICK DOUGLASS
A Maryland slave who
escapes to freedom
in 1838 and soon after
becomes an
abolitionist leader,
campaigning for the
emancipation of all slaves.

ALEXANDER MILTON ROSS
A Canadian naturalist and
abolitionist who is
a friend of John Brown.
During the Civil War he is
a Union Army surgeon
and a secret agent for
President Lincoln.

JOHN BROWN
A ferocious abolitionist
who first fights slavery in
Kansas. He enlists Harriet
in a plan for an armed
rebellion of slaves.
Captured after a failed raid,
he is tried and hanged.

COL. THOMAS W. HIGGINSON
A Unitarian minister and
leading Boston abolitionist,
he is one of John Brown's
"Secret Six."
Harriet's friend and booster,
he leads a black
regiment in South Carolina.

ANTHONY BURNS
The last slave arrested
under the Fugitive Slave Act.
Col. Higginson fails in his
attempt to free Burns from
federal marshals in Boston.
Supporters later buy
his freedom.

JAMES MONTGOMERY
A veteran of the anti-slavery
war in "Bloody Kansas"
and a friend of John Brown,
he commands the
black regiment that
Harriet leads to free slaves
in South Carolina.

GOV. JOHN A. ANDREW
Governor of Massachusetts,
this leading abolitionist
sends Harriet to
South Carolina as an agent
and recruiter of ex-slaves
to serve as spies, scouts,
and soldiers for the Union.

6

BENJAMIN BUTLER
Northern general who decides
that runaway slaves can be
taken into Union forces as
"contraband of war."
His decision comes long
before President Lincoln's
Emancipation Proclamation.

CONTRABANDS
Slaves who escape from their
masters to Union Army
camps, where many enlist.
They are called "contrabands"
because they are viewed as
a form of war loot.
Official freedom comes later.

ELIZABETH VAN LEW
A wealthy Southern lady
who operates a Union spy
ring in Richmond, Virginia.
She uses both black and
white agents and writes
her reports in a secret code
no one ever broke.

**SECRETARY OF STATE
WILLIAM H. SEWARD**
Member of Lincoln's Cabinet
and friend of Harriet. Seward
had a "secret service fund" for
paying spies. As an abolitionist,
he helped Harriet work
on the Underground Railroad.

MARY ELIZABETH BOWSER
Former slave of Van Lew
trained to work in the
Confederate White house,
spying on
President Jefferson Davis.
She is also known
as Mary Jane Richards.

JOHN SCOBELL
A free black who works
as a Union spy,
posing as a slave and
doing odd jobs as he
picks up information.
Like other black spies, he
was ignored by Southerners.

ROBERT SMALLS
A seagoing slave in
Charleston, he takes over
a ship and delivers it
to the Union Navy,
which he then serves.
After the war,
he is elected to Congress.

GENERAL DAVID HUNTER
A Union general who enlists
ex-slaves into the Army in
South Carolina without
Lincoln's permission.
This leads to the creation
of many black regiments in
the Union Army.

"BLACK MOSES" leads men and women out of slavery. Harriet Tubman got this nickname because she led her people to freedom, as did Moses of the Bible.

Black Moses.

HARRIET, THE SLAVE · HARRIET AS BLACK MOSES ·
A COUNTRY DIVIDED: SLAVE AND FREE ·
HARRIET JOINS THE UNION CAUSE · FREDERICK
DOUGLASS'S "TRUE HISTORY" OF THE CIVIL WAR

Long before the Civil War began, Harriet Tubman started her own war against slavery. Born a slave, she worked day after day and year after year on Maryland farms. The daughter of one master whipped her, scarring her for life. Another master fractured her skull. She saw her sisters taken away by slave traders. She was not allowed to learn to read and write.

As the years passed, she began planning ways to escape from her slavery. She knew that many other slaves had managed to flee. She also knew that many had been tracked down, beaten, and brought back in chains. But she decided that freedom was worth whatever she had to do to find it.

On a fall day in 1849, other slaves heard her singing:

> *When that old chariot comes,*
> *I'm gwine to leave you.*
> *I'm bound for the Promised Land,*
> *Friends, I'm gwine to leave you*
> *I'll meet you in the mornin',*
> *When you reach the Promised Land*
> *On the other side of Jordan,*
> *For I'm bound for the Promised Land.*

The song was one of the secret messages that slaves used to pass information to each other, especially when one of them was about to try to journey to freedom. Harriet did not yet know it, but she was learning how to live a secret life. [1]*

When night fell on the day she sang of the Promised Land, Harriet slipped into the darkness

---

*Throughout this book, numbers in brackets correspond to numbers listed chapter by chapter in the Text Notes beginning on page 173.

and headed for freedom, hiding by day, following the North Star by night.

After her escape, she went back again and again to guide other slaves to freedom. She risked her life and her liberty at a time when Northerners and Southerners were trying to find a way to live with the stain of slavery. Slaveholders in the South offered rewards of thousands of dollars to catch this little black woman who carried a gun and was ready to use it.

Her heroic work gradually became known, and she was hailed in the North as "Black Moses" because, like Moses in the Bible, she had led people out of slavery.

The United States was split between the slave states of the South and the free states of the North. In 1861, when the Civil War began, the Union officially divided. Southern states became the Confederate States of America, while the Northern states, including those that came to be known as Border States, remained in the Union (see map, pages 14–15). The Civil War changed Harriet's mission. Instead of trying to help just a few slaves escape to freedom, she joined the Union's cause, devoting her life to gaining freedom for all slaves.

Like Moses in the Bible, Harriet Tubman, as the "Black Moses," worked as a spy. The Moses of the Bible secretly gathered information by sending spies into Canaan, the Promised Land. The Bible says he ordered his spies to go out and "see the land, what it is; and the people that dwelleth therein, whether they be strong or weak, few or many."

Moses was a spymaster—and so was the Black Moses. Harriet Tubman spied for the Union and talked ex-slaves into doing the same, sometimes even going into Confederate territory to help Union soldiers gather information that could win battles. She and all the other African Americans who spied for the Union knew the price of their courage: If they were caught, they could be hanged.

Harriet's work had begun when North and South were at peace. But there was no peace for

6253616151165531214433443361201211154454361656211366355436355436361341346532453424343215363354363366124112411*

---

*Throughout this book, you will find secret messages based on a code used by Elizabeth Van Lew. Use her "cipher square" on page 172 to find out what they say. Then check your answers on the author's Web site: www.tballen.com.

Harriet. She wanted to save all the men, women, and children who still were enslaved. "I have heard their groans and sighs, and seen their tears," she said, "and I would give every drop of blood in my veins to free them."

When the Civil War began, her personal war against slavery became part of the war to preserve the Union. Her spycraft, her cunning mind, her secret ways—now they would be working for the Union Army. She believed that what she was doing would end slavery for all time.

She was not alone. She was one of countless—and usually unknown—African Americans who served the Union as spies. This book is about Harriet, but it is also about some of those other spies who served in what Frederick Douglass, himself a runaway slave, called the "true history" of the Civil War. In that history, he wrote, is the work of "faithful, active, and daring" African Americans who "repeatedly threaded their way through the lines of the rebels, exposing themselves to bullets to convey important information" to the Union Army.

The Union Splits Apart

Six weeks after Abraham Lincoln was elected President in November 1860, South Carolina seceded—withdrew—from the Union. This began the breakup of the United States and the start of the Confederate States of America, also called the Confederacy. Some states followed right away. Others seceded after Confederate guns fired on a Union fort in Charleston, South Carolina, on April 12, 1861. Five Border States—Delaware, Maryland, Kentucky, Missouri, and, in 1863, West Virginia—all had slaves but stayed in the Union.

WASHINGTON
TERRITORY

OREGON

NEV.
TERR.

UTAH
TERRITORY

CALIF.

NEW MEXIC
TERRITOR

Union free state

Union slave state (Border State

Slave state seceding
before Fort Sumter, April 1861

Slave state seceding
after Fort Sumter, April 1861

Territory

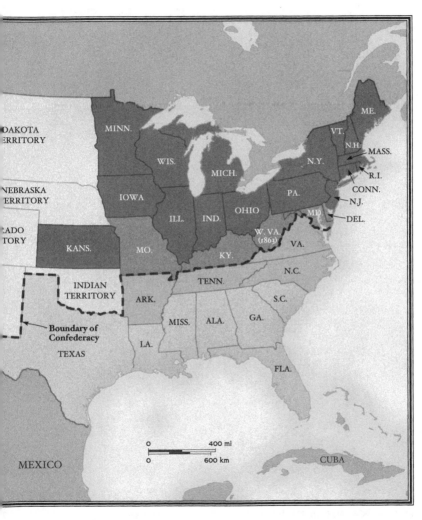

DAKOTA
TERRITORY

NEBRASKA
TERRITORY

COLORADO
TERRITORY

MINN.

WIS.

MICH.

IOWA

ILL.   IND.   OHIO

KANS.

MO.

KY.

ME.

VT.

N.H.

MASS.

N.Y.

R.I.

CONN.

PA.

N.J.

MD.

DEL.

W. VA.
(1863)

VA.

N.C.

TENN.

INDIAN
TERRITORY

ARK.

S.C.

MISS.   ALA.   GA.

Boundary of
Confederacy

LA.

TEXAS

FLA.

0   400 mi

0   600 km

MEXICO

CUBA

15

UNDERGROUND RAILROAD PASSENGERS. Runaway slaves leave a
house where they were secretly given food and shelter and sent on their way.

Chapter 1.

Harriet's Escape.

Mason-Dixon Line · The birth of
Araminta "Minty" Ross · The blow that
changed Minty's life · Minty becomes Harriet ·
Help from the Quakers · Harriet escapes

Back in the days before the United States existed, three British colonies—Delaware, Maryland, and Pennsylvania—could not agree on their boundaries. So British officials sent Charles Mason, an astronomer, and Jeremiah Dixon, a surveyor, to the colonies to solve the problem. From 1763 to 1767, Mason and Dixon surveyed and corrected the boundaries of these three colonies, setting the new boundaries with stone markers. Many stones are still in place.

The line they drew went east-west between Pennsylvania and Maryland and north-south along the Delaware-Maryland-Virginia (Delmarva) Peninsula, which separates Chesapeake and Delaware Bays. It became known as the Mason-Dixon Line. By the early nineteenth century, it was the symbolic boundary between slavery and freedom. To the north was Pennsylvania, which had passed a law abolishing slavery. To the south was Maryland, whose eastern region, the Eastern Shore, ran along the edge of another slave state, Delaware. Although officially Maryland was a slave state, the state was split, with some people opposing slavery. [1]

On a farm near Bucktown, on Maryland's Eastern Shore, Harriet Tubman was born, probably in 1822. Her parents were slaves named Harriet Green and Benjamin Ross. They named their fifth child Araminta Ross. Her nickname was Minty. [2]

Minty Ross was still a child, too young for the fields, when she first felt the pain of a whip, wielded by a woman enraged because Minty did not dust well enough. When Minty was about twelve years old, her master threw a heavy iron weight at a slave suspected of trying to run away.

The weight missed the slave and struck Minty. The blow fractured her skull and knocked her out. When she came to, she was still in a daze. But she went back to work, "with the blood and sweat rolling down my face till I couldn't see." [3]

A WHITE MISTRESS uses a shovel to beat a slave girl, who has no rights.

For the rest of her life, Minty suffered from what that blow did to her brain. She would suddenly fall asleep, sometimes in the middle of a sentence. While working, she would unexpectedly feel extremely tired and struggle to keep on working. Nowadays, doctors would probably say she had epilepsy, but Minty never saw a doctor. She began having visions that seemed to give her glimpses of the future. In some way, the blow to her head helped to shape her because the visions made her believe in herself. She was a young and cruelly treated slave, but something deep inside her was telling her that she was to do great deeds. [4]

She grew up to be strong and smart. "I could tote a flour barrel on one shoulder," she boasted. Her owner often hired her out to other masters on nearby corn and tobacco farms and in the oak and pine forests that added timber crops to the slave owners' vast estates.

At about the age of twenty-two, she married a free African American named John Tubman, perhaps hoping that someday he could buy her freedom. The marriage did not free her. She was still a slave, still a person who could be bought and sent somewhere else, far from her family. Minty dropped her nickname, took her mother's name, and became known as Harriet Tubman. For about five years she worked, sometimes in fields, sometimes in forests, where she hauled logs or chopped wood. She could chop half a cord a day.*

The death of her master in 1849 worried Harriet, for she feared that his widow would try to raise money by selling slaves to the highest bidder. Years before, two of Harriet's sisters had been

*A cord is a stack of logs measuring 4 x 4 x 8 feet.

SLAVES GO TO MARKET, where they will be auctioned off to the highest bidders. Parents were often sold to one owner, children to another.

sold and forced to leave their children behind. Slave traders often bought slaves to work in the cotton plantations of Georgia and Mississippi, a fate dreaded by Maryland slaves.

Harriet took her fears to her husband and said they should flee to the North. John Tubman

Although tenaciously delivered amid the are gradually melt-d parcel of the com-w dwell. This fact United States, where existed since the Re-Israel are, in every prominent in all the of life. The door of ually to them as to ds. They need no from public observa-openly, that God who the wilderness. If zens of New Orleans, y of our most distin-e professions, or in re of the Jewish per-ssidered as intruding mention one Israelite uile"—who has, dur-city, of nearly half a ation for benevolence proudest christian

be accommodated. For sale by
EDWARD McINALL,
(Authorised agent) 42 Market st.,
oct 5   Wilmington, Del,

THREE HUNDRED DOLLARS REWARD.

RANAWAY from the subscriber, on Monday the 17th ult., three negroes, named as follows: HARRY, aged about 19 years, has on one side of his neck a wen, just under the ear; he is of a dark chesnut color, about 5 feet 8 or 9 inches high; BEN, aged about 25 years, is very quick to speak when spoken to, he is of a chesnut color, and about six feet high—MINTY, aged about 27 years, is of a chesnut color, fine looking, and about 5 feet high. One hundred dollars reward will be given for each of the above named negroes, if taken out of the State, and $50 each if taken in the State. They must be lodged in Baltimore, Easton, or Cambridge Jail, in Maryland.
ELIZA ANN BRODESS.
Near Bucktown, Dorchester county Md.
oct 5—3w   [Cambridge Chron.]

LONG SHAWLS—W. JONES, No. 55 Market street, has now on hand a splendid as-

ware, on SATURDAY, BER next, at 2 o'clock, scribed REAL ESTATE All that Lot, piece or p Buildings thereon er being in the City, Co bounded and described as a stake standing on the street at forty nine feet also the corner of the L Samuel Carnahan, dece Chandler, thence with a eight degrees, West eight other corner stake, bei William Chandler's Lot, degrees West sixteen fee half or an inch to a corn fifty eight degrees East, with the first mentioned eighty two feet six inch of Orange street, throu feet ten inch wide alley, ley in common for ever, North thirty two degrees inches and one half of an ginning, containing thirt and a half feet of Land, being the same premises Isaiah Stair, (butcher,)

WANTED: HARRIET. A newspaper advertisement, paid for by her owner, offers a $100 reward for Harriet Tubman, who was then known as Minty.

refused. But Harriet began making plans to escape and talked her brothers Henry and Ben into joining her. On September 17, 1849, the three ran away. Their owner bought a newspaper advertisement offering a $300 reward for their return. The advertisement says "Minty" was "about 27 years, is of a chestnut color, fine looking, and about 5 feet high." The advertisement also appeared in *The Gazette* in Wilmington, Delaware. This shows that the slave owner believed the most likely escape route was across Delaware, then through Wilmington to a free state (as states that forbade slavery were called). He was right.

Somewhere on their flight to freedom, the two brothers lost their nerve. They headed back to slavery and forced their sister to return with them and take their punishment. A few days later, Harriet ran away again—alone. This time she did not turn back. "There was one of two things I had a *right* to, liberty, or death," Harriet later said. "If I could not have one, I would have the other, for no man should take me alive. I should fight for my liberty as long as my strength lasted." [5]

Harriet traveled by night, stopping before dawn at a "safe house," where an anti-slavery family broke Maryland law by helping her. Many of these people were Quakers (members of The Religious Society of Friends). Quakers were against slavery, and they knew how to help slaves escape on secret routes to the North. [6]

"We fed, we clothed, and directed them on-wards toward the North Star," wrote a Maryland Quaker. "We often conveyed them to other Friends, but they often traveled alone, through swamps and byways. Public roads were avoided. We sometimes hired trusty colored men to go with them."

Harriet kept following the North Star,* moving from one safe house to the next until she reached Wilmington. There, Thomas Garrett, a Quaker who ran an iron and blacksmithing business, secretly helped slaves head north—just as his parents had done when he was a child. Garrett and other men and women helped more than 2,700 slaves pass through Delaware to freedom in Pennsylvania.

In 1848, the year before Harriet fled, Garrett had been tried and convicted in New Castle, Delaware, of aiding in the escape of a family of Maryland slaves. U.S. Supreme Court Chief Justice Roger B. Taney showed how important he thought the case to be by sitting as the judge in the trial. He fined Garrett $5,400, then an enormous sum that left Garrett almost penniless. After hearing the sentence, Garrett used the Quaker way of speaking to say to the judge: "Thou has left me

*Like most country people, she knew that the two stars opposite the handle of the Drinking Gourd (for whites, the Big Dipper) pointed to the North Star.

without a dollar...I say to thee and to all in this courtroom, that if anyone knows a fugitive who wants shelter...send him to Thomas Garrett and he will befriend him." [7]

Whether Harriet met Garrett on her flight northward is not known. But she and he later worked together on the Underground Railroad, the secret delivery system that got her across the state line to Pennsylvania. At the moment she crossed that line between slavery and freedom, she later said, "I looked at my hands to see if I was the same person, now I was free. There was such a glory over everything, the sun came like gold through the trees and over the fields, and I felt like I was in heaven."

SPECIAL DELIVERY. Ex-slave Henry Brown, who shipped himself from Richmond, arrives in Philadelphia after twenty-six hours in a box.

Chapter 2

The Underground Railroad.

ORIGINS OF THE UNDERGROUND RAILROAD ·
"THE BRANDED HAND" · THE FUGITIVE SLAVE ACT ·
HARRIET THE SLAVE SMUGGLER · ABOLITIONIST THREATS ·
STATION MASTER DOUGLASS · ALEXANDER ROSS AND
THE CANADIAN UNDERGROUND RAILROAD

Since slavery's earliest days in America, people who hated slavery had helped slaves escape to the North. In the early days, the helpers had no name for their secret escape routes, but, because the fleeing slaves did their best not to be seen, it was said they were traveling "underground." When railroad lines started appearing in America in the 1820s, the term "Underground Railroad" began to catch on. Escape routes were called "lines." Houses where escaping slaves ("packages" or "freight") got shelter were "stations." And the people who helped the freight get from one station to the next were "conductors." Men and women like the Garretts, who watched over the Underground Railroad in an area, were called "station masters."

People who supported slavery considered the Underground Railroad a criminal organization whose members were "slave stealers." Because slaves were considered property, anyone helping a slave escape in Southern states could be arrested for theft and severely punished.

Jonathan Walker, a ship captain, was tried in Florida in 1844 for trying to take seven runaway slaves to the British West Indies, where slavery was outlawed. Walker was found guilty and sentenced to be fined, jailed—and branded. He was the first man in American history to be branded by order of a federal judge. A blacksmith made a special branding iron, which was heated in the courtroom. Walker's right hand was raised above his head and tied to a pillar so spectators could get a good view. Then a U.S. marshal pressed the iron against Walker's palm and branded *SS*—for slave stealer—on it.

SS FOR SLAVE STEALER was branded on the hand of Jonathan Walker, a ship captain who tried to smuggle slaves to the British West Indies. Abolitionists saw SS as initials for Slave Savior.

The horrible event inspired John Greenleaf Whittier to write a poem, "The Branded Hand." In the poem, Whitter predicted that the "branded palm shall prophesy/Salvation for the slave." Whittier was an abolitionist—a person who wanted to abolish slavery.

During the same time, the U.S. Congress was trying to deal with slavery. Southern states were threatening to leave the Union if the Northern states outlawed slavery. Abolitionists believed that if slavery continued, the United States would be torn apart anyway. They were right. Month by month, year by year, America was moving toward civil war.

In 1850, the year after Harriet escaped slavery, Congress passed the Fugitive Slave Act, a federal law that made a criminal of anyone who helped escaping slaves—or refused to help government agents chasing slaves. The new law did not stop the Underground Railroad or Harriet Tubman.

On Harriet's first trip as an Underground Railroad conductor, she returned to Maryland and managed the escape of her niece and the niece's two children. Then, in September 1851, she slipped back to her birthplace, hoping to guide her husband to the North. But John Tubman had remarried and wanted to stay. Harriet left him behind for good but kept on with her mission as conductor, leading many others to freedom.

She made it clear to the slaves she helped that she was in charge and had to be strictly obeyed. She had a gun and warned that anyone who decided to return would be shot as a traitor. A writer once asked Harriet if she really would have shot anyone who wanted to turn back. "Yes," she said. "If he was weak enough to give out, he'd be weak enough to betray us all, and all who helped us; and do you think I'd let so many die just for one coward man?"

Harriet became a celebrity among abolitionists in the North and a wanted criminal in the South. From 1851 to the beginning of the Civil War, Harriet made about a dozen trips to Maryland and guided about seventy people to freedom. She told many more slaves how to escape. "I never lost a passenger," she said. [1]

In her life as a smuggler of slaves, Harriet learned some of the basic spy procedures that today's intelligence agents call "tradecraft." For example, if two spies must meet, they try to set up a meeting in a way that puts only one in danger. Harriet did this by having escaping slaves meet her seven or eight miles from their cabins. Chances were that anyone spotting their escape would capture them before they reached Harriet.

She also used the "cutout." When a cautious spy wants to give a message or document to a contact or a partner, he or she does not set up a meeting.

Instead, arrangements are made for a third person—a cutout—to make the pickup from one spy and the delivery to the other. In this way, if a spy is being followed, he or she does not lead the follower to the second spy. [2]

Harriet's work on the Underground Railroad made her an enemy of slave catchers and their allies, the dozens of slave traders who prospered by buying Maryland slaves and shipping them South. For years, slave catchers looked for her in hopes of collecting rewards—one as high as $12,000—for her capture. They used specially trained dogs to track runaway slaves, but neither the catchers nor their dogs ever found anyone who was in her care. The slave catchers' repeated failures added to her legend. Boston abolitionists especially honored her, often asking her to tell her Underground Railroad stories at fund-raising meetings. She sometimes spoke under a false name and was well protected by her friends in the North. [3]

Abolitionists' funds produced anti-slavery newspapers and pamphlets that poured into the North and South. Even Northerners were shocked by the hatred and violence that peppered abolitionists' writings. One leading abolitionist, for instance, said that "every slaveholder has forfeited his right to live." Concerned about such threats, the state legislators in Connecticut, Maine, and New Hampshire introduced bills to restrain abolitionist publications.

Abolitionists continued to publish their views and to disobey the Fugitive Slave Act. They also extended the Underground Railroad

TRACKED BY SLAVE HUNTERS and their dog, a slave escapes. With the help of the Underground Railroad, he may make it to freedom in Canada.

into Canada, beyond the reach of federal law. Harriet now began leading ex-slaves (including her brothers) all the way to Canada. For about six years, she lived part of the time in St. Catharines,

Canada—a refuge for escapees—and part of the time in western New York State, site of many stations on the Underground Railroad's lines into Canada. One of those stations, in Rochester, was run by abolitionist leader Frederick Douglass. He and Harriet had been born slaves in the same Maryland county. He had run away in 1838. His station in Rochester was often a stop for the slaves Harriet sent on to Canada.

One of the best Underground Railroad workers in Canada was Alexander Milton Ross of Belleville, Ontario, a doctor and a naturalist. Ross began his own crusade to help escaped slaves after reading *Uncle Tom's Cabin*, an anti-slavery novel written by Harriet Beecher Stowe. He visited many of the ex-slaves living in Canada, "heard heart-rending stories," and saw "the indelible marks of the lash and branding-iron upon their bodies."

Before heading south on his personal crusade, Ross met with several abolitionists in Boston and in Philadelphia. Warning him of the dangers he faced, one of them gave him a pistol. Ross managed to meet with slaves in the Deep South by giving himself what modern spies would call a "cover." He introduced himself to plantation owners as a bird-watcher and got permission to roam around their property. Because Southerners looked at Canada as pro-South, Ross was usually treated as a welcome stranger. While supposedly looking for birds, Ross talked to slaves and told them about escape routes to Canada.

Ross was called an "abductor," rather than a conductor, because he did not lead slaves to freedom but urged them to escape. He spent months in an area, secretly—and dangerously—developing friendships with slaves on plantations in Virginia, Tennessee, South Carolina, Louisiana, Mississippi, Georgia, and Alabama. When Ross had arranged an escape, he sent word to conductors in Ohio and Pennsylvania that he was shipping "hardware," which meant male slaves, or "dry goods," which meant female slaves. [4]

Ross met Harriet Tubman in Canada, and, like her, he would become a secret agent for the Union during a war that, in 1858, was rapidly approaching.

SLAVES KILL MASTERS and their families in Haiti in 1791. The rebellion frightened American slave owners, especially where whites were outnumbered.

Chapter 3.

Slave Revolts.

SLAVE REVOLT IN HAITI · DENMARK VESEY'S
CHARLESTON UPRISING · NAT TURNER'S
VIRGINIA REVOLT · WILLIAM LLOYD GARRISON AND
THE LIBERATOR · BLOODY KANSAS · BEECHER'S BIBLES
VS. BORDER RUFFIANS · JOHN BROWN AT POTTAWATOMIE

For Harriet Tubman, Alexander Milton Ross, and other abolitionists in Canada and the United States, by 1850 the war against slavery was changing from a war of pamphlets and speeches to a war of guns and blood. Both Southerners and Northerners were talking about taking a path to violence. And nothing was feared more in the South than a slave uprising.

The bloodiest revolt had begun in Haiti, on the Caribbean island of Hispaniola, in 1791. Nearly 500,000 slaves warred against the French in a struggle that ended with Haiti's declaration of independence in 1804. Word of the massacres spread throughout the American South, especially in the rice-growing areas of South Carolina, where slaves outnumbered whites eighty or ninety to one. South Carolina had more slaves than any other state.

In May 1822, a slave in South Carolina told his master incredible news: A revolt of thousands of slaves around Charleston was to erupt in July, led by Denmark Vesey. He was a free man and a leader in a black Methodist church. [1]

Authorities rounded up suspects and tried them in a special court in Charleston. Vesey and thirty-four others were hanged, with federal troops guarding the gallows. Little publicity was given to the trial because Charleston officials did not want to spread the news that slaves were capable of planning revolts.

Then, in 1831, came a revolt that did happen. Nat Turner, a slave in southeastern Virginia, recruited several fellow slaves to join him in a rebellion. After killing Turner's master and the rest of his family, the band murdered nearly sixty white people, mostly women and children. For weeks, federal

PLOTTING A SLAVE REVOLT. Nat Turner recruits other slaves. Believing that "signs in the heavens" would guide him, he took an eclipse of the sun in 1831 as a signal and launched the revolt by killing his master and his family.

troops, Virginia militia, and civilians bent on vengeance hunted down Turner, killing scores of other slaves, most of them innocent. Turner and twenty others were tried and hanged.

Angry, fearful Southerners accused northern abolitionists of stirring up the slaves and inspiring the revolt. By what Southerners saw as more than a coincidence, William Lloyd Garrison, a leading Massachusetts abolitionist, had started publishing his newspaper, *The Liberator*, seven months before Turner started his revolt. Most slave owners did not think that slaves were capable of organizing their own rebellion. So they blamed Garrison.

Abolitionists were getting more and more violent in their campaign against slavery and the federal government's enforcement of the Fugitive Slave Act. Congress had been trying to avoid war by balancing slave states against free states, meaning that for every territory entering the Union as a free state, another territory entered as a state that allowed slavery. But then Congress passed the decision to the people, allowing each new state to vote for or against slavery.

When the Kansas Territory opened up in 1854, abolitionists raised funds for hundreds of families to move from free states to Kansas. There, they could vote against slavery in their new state. Backing the ballots were boxes of rifles, sent to Kansas by Massachusetts abolitionists. The weapons were called "Beecher's Bibles," named after Henry Ward Beecher, a New York clergyman who said that slaveholders might understand a rifle better than a Bible. (Henry was Harriet Beecher Stowe's brother.)

After hearing about the abolitionists' plan to tip the Kansas vote to make it a free state, a leading Missouri politician told his pro-slavery supporters: "I advise you, one and all to...vote at the point of the bowie-knife and revolver." Thousands of armed Missourians rode across the border to illegally cast votes for slavery.

They won, but the election had so many fake voters that another election was held. Again the "Border Ruffians" from Missouri rode in and voted for slavery, winning the election even though they did not live in Kansas. The new, pro-slave legislature passed a law forbidding anyone to write or speak out against slavery. Under another law, anyone who helped a slave to escape could be hanged. [2]

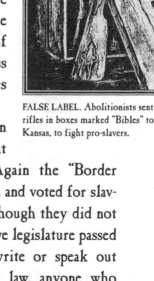

FALSE LABEL. Abolitionists sent rifles in boxes marked "Bibles" to Kansas, to fight pro-slavers.

HEADING FOR TROUBLE, caravans of gun-toting men enter Kansas from Missouri. These pro-slavers came to be known as "Border Ruffians." Raiding Kansas and battling abolitionists, they fought to make Kansas a slave state.

The Kansas slavery war roared on. In May 1856, more than 500 armed pro-slavers attacked Lawrence, a new Kansas town founded by abolitionists. They burned down a hotel, smashed the presses of abolitionist newspapers, wrecked homes and stores, and killed a man.

John Brown was one of those abolitionists who saw Kansas as a battleground, where bullets, not ballots, would decide the issue of slavery. He and five of his sons had come to the territory from Ohio in 1855 to keep it from becoming a slave state. Brown reacted to the Lawrence attack by leading seven men—including four of his sons and a son-in-law—to the town of Pottawatomie. There, they dragged a pro-slaver and his two sons from their home and hacked them to death. That night they killed two more pro-slavers.

U.S. Army peacekeepers and pro-slaver posses pursued Brown, but he escaped, thanks to the help of supporters. The events in Kansas convinced him that the only way to end slavery was to lead an armed slave revolt against pro-slavers. Harriet Tubman would be among his recruits.

WARRIOR AGAINST SLAVERY, John Brown glares out of a portrait that shows his passion and fierce faith in himself as a leader of a slave army.

Chapter 4.

John Brown Meets the General.

Funding the slave army · John Brown meets
Harriet · Harriet's dream · "General" Tubman ·
John Brown's constitution · Harriet meets
Colonel Higginson · The slave army gathers

Brown fled Kansas, where he faced hanging
as a murderer, and headed for upstate New
York. There and in New England he asked
abolitionists for money to raise a slave army and
to pay for hundreds of "pikes" that he had
ordered from a Connecticut blacksmith. The
Brown-designed pike had a two-edged blade, ten
inches wide, mounted on a pole six feet long.
Brown believed that the pikes were better
weapons than rifles for slaves because the slaves
would not need any special training to use them in
battle. To disguise the pikes, the poles were to be

shipped as pitchfork handles and the blades in separate packages labeled "hardware."

Brown continued on to Canada, where he spent time with Alexander Milton Ross, the "abductor" wanted as a criminal throughout the South. After talking to Brown and getting a pistol from him, Ross disappeared, probably into the South. Later, during the Civil War he would be a spy working directly for President Lincoln. [1]

Canada was also where Brown and Harriet Tubman were brought together by several abolitionists, including Frederick Douglass and a group of rich supporters of John Brown known as the Secret Six. [2]

Brown had suggested that he meet Harriet in a St. Catharines hotel. Instead, fearing that he might be under surveillance as a wanted outlaw, she invited him to her home, saying that she would have friends there who would protect him.

Harriet and other ex-slaves heard Brown reveal his plan: He would build a stronghold somewhere in the Allegheny Mountains. Slaves from Southern plantations were to flee to this

A PRO-SLAVERY MOB tries to stop Frederick Douglass from making a speech to abolitionists. Douglass captured audiences with stories of his life as a slave and as a station master on the Underground Railroad.

stronghold, where they, along with free black and white supporters, would make a stand against slavery. He predicted that the revolt would grow and spread, uniting all slaves into a crusade that would bring down slavery.

Before Harriet met Brown, she had had the same dream again and again: "I was in a wilderness

HARRIET'S DREAM. Again and again Harriet dreamed of a snake whose head changed to the head of an old man "with a long white beard." Then she met John Brown—and recognized him as the man in her dream.

sort of place, all rocks and bushes, when a big snake raised its head from behind a rock, and while I looked, it changed into the head of an old man with a long white beard on his chin, and he looked at me, wishful like, just as if he was going to speak to me."

When she first saw Brown, she later said, he looked exactly like the bearded man in her vision. And when Brown saw Harriet, he believed that he had found exactly the person he needed for his revolt. He repeatedly called her "General Tubman" and, said one of his biographers, "his brave and daring spirit found ready sympathy in her courageous heart."

This was a time when women were second-class citizens: They were not allowed to vote. They were rarely employed in any but unskilled jobs. And they were usually looked upon as weak, helpless human beings. But in Harriet Tubman, an African-American woman barely five feet tall and unable to read or write, John Brown saw such courage that he could not think of her as a woman, even a superwoman. He insisted on using *he* and *him* when referring to her. He believed that she "could command an army...He [Harriet] is the most of a man naturally that I ever met with. There is abundant material here and of the right quality."

John Brown changed Harriet's life. As an Underground Railroad conductor, she had worked with peace-loving Quakers and abolitionists. Brown, sneering at "milk and water" abolitionists, introduced Harriet to the violent world of pikes and killing. She began recruiting ex-slaves for his army, and he donated money for her work helping ex-slaves in New York and Canada.

To carry out his plan, Brown called a secret convention in May 1858 at Chatham, Ontario, about 180 miles west of St. Catharines. At the convention, John Brown presented a constitution that had been written in the home of Frederick Douglass. The constitution guaranteed equality for both black and white citizens and set up a government organized to go to war against slave-holding enemies.

Neither Douglass nor Harriet appeared at the convention. Harriet may not have had money for the trip. She certainly backed Brown, for she spoke often to abolitionists, urging them to donate to Brown's cause.

Harriet didn't know the details of Brown's plans for the revolt, only that it was to begin with a raid in Virginia. She suggested that the best day to start was the Fourth of July—a holiday that had special meaning to slaves and abolitionists. To them, celebration of the signing of the Declaration of Independence was a cruel joke. As Frederick Douglass put it, "What, to the American slave, is your 4th of July? I answer....To him, your celebration is a sham." [3]

Brown probably would have launched his plan in July 1858, but he was talking too much. A supporter warned him that many people were aware of what should have been secret information. Brown learned that one of his trusted lieutenants had betrayed him by revealing the plan to members of Congress. Brown went into hiding and decided to postpone the revolt.

Restless, he returned to Kansas. He led a raid across the Missouri line, killed a slaveholder, and freed eleven slaves. Again he dodged pursuers, and, after a perilous journey of eighty-two freezing winter days, Brown got the slaves—and a baby born along the way—all the way to Canada.

Late in May 1859, Brown reappeared in Boston, where he met Harriet again. He brought her to the home of an abolitionist and introduced her as "one of the best and bravest persons on this continent."

At this time she also met Thomas Wentworth Higginson, who knew about Brown's plans for a revolt, was raising funds for him, and was involved in a plot to ship rifles to Kansas. He was well-known among abolitionists as the man who had led a Boston mob in a futile attempt to free Anthony Burns, an escaped slave who was being held under the Fugitive Slave Act. [4]

By the time Harriet met Higginson in 1859, she was as much a wanted criminal as John Brown. At a July 4 meeting of the Massachusetts Anti-Slavery Society, Higginson protected Harriet by not revealing her name, introducing her only as "a conductor on the Underground Railroad."

❊

In July 1859, Brown decided the time was right for his raid. Using the name Isaac Smith, he rented a vacant farmhouse in Maryland, across the river from Harpers Ferry, Virginia (now West Virginia). The town, at the junction of the Shenandoah and Potomac Rivers, was the site of a federal rifle factory and arsenal.

CAPTURED SLAVE Anthony Burns, standing next to a federal marshal in a Boston courthouse, gestures to a mob trying to free him. The leader of the mob was Harriet's friend and John Brown supporter Thomas Wentworth Higginson.

For weeks, men and arms arrived by night at the farm and were hidden away. In August, Brown met secretly with Frederick Douglass at a stone quarry not far from the farmhouse. After raving about his plans, Brown pleaded: "Come with me, Douglass...When I strike, the bees will begin to swarm, and I shall want you to help hive them."

JOHN BROWN'S FOLLOWERS slip into the Maryland farmhouse that
served as the headquarters for his 1859 raid on Harpers Ferry. Brown told
Harriet that the raid would launch a revolt of slaves against their masters.

Douglass refused, believing that Brown had no
chance to succeed. Shields Green, a former slave
from South Carolina, had accompanied Douglass.
Green said, "I believe I'll go with the old man."

Brown was hoping that Harriet would join him
and, as General Tubman, fight in the opening battle
of the great slave revolt. But Harriet did not arrive.
No one knew why then, and still no one knows why.

Harriet spoke to many people about her life and her deeds, but she never explained why she did not go with John Brown. Some who talked to her believed that she was prevented from traveling because she was suffering from the sickness—probably epilepsy—that had so often unexpectedly attacked her. Or, like Douglass, she may have learned enough of John Brown's plan to decide that it would be a disaster.

Whatever her reason, it could certainly not be because she was afraid of guns and violence. She was fearless, as she would soon show once again.

FEDERAL TROOPS storm the building where John Brown, his sons, and
other raiders were trapped after their failed attack on the Harpers Ferry arsenal.

Chapter 5.

Trouble at Harpers Ferry.

ROBERT E. LEE IS DISPATCHED TO HARPERS FERRY ·
J. E. B. STUART'S MARINES VS. JOHN BROWN'S RAIDERS ·
LETTERS LINK HARRIET TO JOHN BROWN ·
JOHN BROWN'S TRIAL

On October 17, 1859, J. E. B. ("Jeb") Stuart, a lieutenant in the U.S. Army, went to the Virginia home of Lieutenant Colonel Robert E. Lee and handed him a sealed note from the Secretary of War. Lee met with him and then went to the White House, where President William Buchanan ordered Lee to go to Harpers Ferry, Virginia. Something strange and dangerous was happening there: A band of armed men had taken over the federal arsenal and might be trying to start a slave revolt. [1]

Lee did not yet know that on the night before,

John Brown had led twenty-one followers, including three of his sons and five African Americans, from his Maryland farmhouse to Harpers Ferry. Armed with rifles and the pikes that Brown had designed, they seized the arsenal with its stock of rifles and took control of other places in town. The first man to die was a freed slave who worked at the railroad depot. One of the raiders shot him when he refused an order. Another band of raiders broke into the nearby home of Lewis Washington, a retired Army colonel and great-grandnephew of George Washington, and took him hostage.

About the same time that Robert E. Lee was being handed the sealed letter, Harriet Tubman was having breakfast with friends in New York City. Suddenly, her heart began pounding. For some reason, she later told friends, she thought again of the dream she had so often had about the snake with John Brown's head on it. She suddenly felt that Brown was in trouble. There were two smaller heads in her dream—his sons! Trouble for them, too. Soon, she said, we will be hearing some bad news about John Brown.

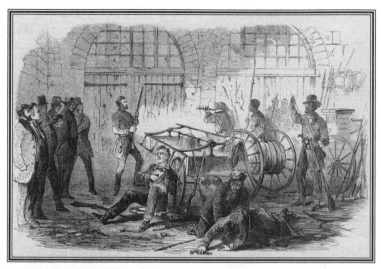

REFUSING TO SURRENDER, John Brown and his raiders defend their position inside the firehouse. Hostages stand along one wall. Men lie dying. Against the opposite wall are pikes, weapons Brown had designed for his army of ex-slaves.

Lee, still in civilian clothes, headed by train for Harpers Ferry along with Stuart. The U.S. Army troops and Marines whom Lee would command were already on the way.

By the time Lee arrived, he had learned that a man calling himself Isaac Smith was the leader of the group. They had taken dozens of hostages. After gunfights with militiamen and townspeople,

BURSTING THROUGH THE DOOR, troops find John Brown still alive and fighting. An officer slashed him with a sword, then captured him and four others. Five of Brown's followers escaped, finding safety in Canada.

the invaders were holed up in a firehouse near the arsenal gate. Brown and his men were surrounded, but they kept firing.

Lee sent Stuart to the door of the firehouse under a white flag. Stuart instantly recognized "Smith" as John Brown, the killer Stuart had hunted in 1856, when he was stationed with the

U.S. Army in Kansas. While Brown tried to talk Stuart into a compromise, the hostage Lewis Washington shouted, "Never mind us, fire!"

Brown, with one son dead and another dying, refused to surrender. Marines battered down the door. One of the raiders shot and killed a Marine. Brown, wounded, was captured, along with four other raiders. Twelve of Brown's men, including Frederick Douglass' friend Shields Green, were dead. Five escaped and eventually reached Canada.

In New York, Harriet got the news, spread through the nation by a new wonder—America's growing telegraph network. The first rumors said Brown was dead. Then came the true report that he had been wounded and captured. Harriet was relieved, but she knew there was trouble ahead for her.

Back in Harpers Ferry, Lee learned that Brown and his raiders had been living on a farm across the Potomac River in Maryland. Stuart and a party of Marines searched the farmhouse. They found letters and other documents that showed Brown had been in contact with the Secret Six.

Only one of the Secret Six did not panic or flee. Calmly, the Reverend Thomas Wentworth Higginson began organizing a gang to free Brown by storming the jail where he was being held.

One of the searchers in the farmhouse picked up a letter dated June 4, 1859. It said that Brown "is desirous of getting some one to go to Canada, and collect recruits for him among the fugitives—with Harriet Tubman or alone, as the case may be."

Like Higginson, Harriet did not panic. Linked now by their cool reaction to the John Brown raid, Higginson and Harriet would later be linked by other raids in another place.

John Brown, charged with murder, criminal conspiracy with slaves, and treason against the state of Virginia, was put on trial in a heavily guarded courthouse in Charlestown, Virginia (now Charles Town, West Virginia). Harriet had friends read to her about the trial day after day. She is said to have memorized Brown's long final speech to the court in which he declared, "I deny everything but what I have all along admitted, the design on my part to free the slaves."

Higginson's rescue plans fell through. John Brown was hanged on December 2, 1859. [2]

Higginson did not give up. He sent a message to Kansas asking James Montgomery for help in saving two other jailed raiders from the gallows. Montgomery, who had worked alongside Brown in Kansas, arrived with several men. One of them went

CONDEMNED TO DEATH in a trial he said was fair, John Brown leaves the courthouse. An artist imagined this baby-kissing moment.

into Charlestown and staggered around the streets as if he were drunk. He was arrested and jailed for the night. In jail he managed to speak to the two members of Brown's band. They urged the would-be rescuers to call off the planned jailbreak because there were too many guards and soldiers.

Higginson, Montgomery, and their men disappeared, and the raiders were hanged on schedule. [3]

❋

John Brown left only vague outlines of his plans, but enough information was spread to give us an idea of what he intended to do—and what role he wanted Harriet Tubman to play. Brown had poured over maps of the South and even checked census records to find where there were large populations of slaves. He learned the routes of the Underground Railroad and studied military operations and the history of the slave revolt in Haiti. He seemed to have pictured in his mind two ways to end slavery: He would start a revolt and collect his forces in a mountain stronghold. Or, he would someday return to Kansas and take over that state, driving out the slaveholders and making Kansas a sanctuary for ex-slaves.

If the raid on Harpers Ferry had succeeded, Brown and his followers would have hidden in the mountains that tower over the town. Slaves and free blacks from the area would have made their way to Brown's hideout. The gathering of fugitive slaves was the first step of his plan for armed revolt.

Some historians believe that a number of African Americans were moving to join Brown as he was invading Harpers Ferry. Some slaves in the area mysteriously died around that time. They may have been murdered because their masters believed they were planning to join Brown.

Brown's plan called for the movement of many slaves. Imagine, say, fifty or one hundred slaves fleeing a plantation all at once and joining Brown's revolt. That dream did not end with Brown's death. Others would take up the cause. The time would come when Harriet Tubman would find herself carrying out activities that resembled Brown's plan in amazing detail.

WARNING OF SLAVE CATCHERS, abolitionists put up posters like this one in Boston in 1851 to foil the Fugitive Slave Act.

Chapter 6.

The "Old Colored Woman."

EDMUND RUFFIN'S SOUTHERN "FIRE-EATERS"
FAN THE FLAMES OF SECESSION · CIVIL WAR LOOMS ·
HARRIET'S SURPRISE VISIT TO TROY · CHARLES NALLE
ESCAPES, IS CAUGHT, AND ESCAPES AGAIN

News of the Harpers Ferry raid spread through the country, dispiriting abolitionists in the North and rallying pro-slavery forces in the South. Edmund Ruffin, a Virginia plantation owner, managed to get some of John Brown's pikes that had been found near Harpers Ferry. Ruffin was one of a group of Southerners known as "fire-eaters" because of their fanatic belief that the South could keep its slaves only by separating—*seceding*—from the Union and becoming a new nation.

Ruffin carried a pike around on his travels and

NIGHTMARE FOR SOUTHERNERS. The discovery of John Brown's pikes frightened slaveholders, who imagined facing ex-slaves armed with them.

sent pikes to officials in the South as samples of "the favors designed for us by our Northern brethren." Southern politicians and newspapers wrote sensational stories recalling the Nat Turner revolt and raising fears of abolitionist-led insurrections. A Virginia newspaper said that thousands of men "who, a month ago, scoffed at the idea of

[seceding from] the Union as a madman's dream...
now hold the opinion that its days are numbered."

The governor of South Carolina, where slaves
far outnumbered landowners, warned of "secret
emissaries inciting our slaves to insubordination
and insurrection." South Carolina legislators,
remembering the feared 1822 uprising, passed laws
prohibiting abolitionists from stirring up slaves.
The lawmakers even forbade the use of agents posing as traveling salesmen or circus performers.

South Carolinians put the word *secession*
into political debates that were going on throughout the nation as 1859 came to an end. Many in the
North and the South believed that a civil war
already had begun. As a Virginia witness to John
Brown's raid later wrote, "Then and there the first
shots were fired and the first blood shed."

The threats of Southern politicians did not
frighten Harriet Tubman. She was more convinced
than ever that the only way to end slavery was
through armed rebellion by slaves and ex-slaves.
And one day in April 1860, she got a chance to act as
the General that John Brown recognized her to be.

According to what she later told people who were writing about her life, she happened to be in the right place at the right time. But there may be more to the event than a mere coincidence. There is no way to know for sure.

When a spy or a suspected spy does something mysterious, spymasters try to solve the mystery by a method that people in the spy world call "walking back the cat." (You can see why they call it that if you have ever tried to figure out what a cat was up to.) The spymasters begin by going back to some place or some moment that provides definite information. Then they try to move on to the next piece of definite information. Usually, as the trackers move further and further from the starting point, they are dealing with less and less reliable information.

The starting point for this Harriet Tubman mystery is Troy, New York. Troy is a river town about four miles up the Hudson from Albany. By Harriet's account, she was at her home in Auburn, New York, when Gerrit Smith, one of John Brown's Secret Six, asked her to come to Boston to speak at a conference. On her way, she later said, she decided to stop at a cousin's home in Troy, and that is how she happened to be there on April 27, 1860, for what would be her first public battle against slavery.

Whether by chance, on purpose, or through information from Smith and other Brown supporters, Harriet was in Troy on the day when a runaway slave named Charles Nalle was about to be taken back to his master. Nalle had escaped from Virginia in 1858 and had been working odd jobs in Troy until he was captured on April 27. He was taken to a building that held a bank and the office of the U.S. Commissioner who was in charge of handling fugitive slave cases.

What happened next was told first in newspapers of the day and later in biographies of Harriet published during her lifetime. The newspapers told of the exploits of "an old colored woman," who first appeared at the window of the second-floor room where Nalle was being held. Harriet later told her biographer, Sarah H. Bradford, that the old woman was Harriet in disguise.

HARRIET TO THE RESCUE! Disguised as an old woman, Harriet Tubman looks down from a building in Troy, New York, where Charles Nalle, a runaway slave, is held. To free him, she defied federal marshals and urged on a mob.

The newspaper stories tell how the woman gave some kind of signal to the crowd below—an indication that Harriet was not there by coincidence, because people in the crowd seemed to have been expecting the signal.

"The scene became instantaneously one of great excitement," the Troy *Daily Times* reported.

"The moment the officers reached the sidewalk, they were surrounded by the crowd, the inner-circle of which was composed of resolute colored men who at once began a vigorous attempt to rescue the prisoner. The city policemen were soon separated from the other officers...in the midst of a crowd perhaps of two thousand persons, who were swaying to and fro like billows, shouting, laughing, swearing, and fighting."

The "old colored woman" was now in the street, "continually exclaiming, 'Give us liberty or give us death,' and with vehement gesticulations urging on the rescuers. Here the scene became intensely exciting. Revolvers were drawn, knives brandished, colored women rushed into the thickest of the fray, the venerable Molly Pitcher of the occasion was fighting like a demon, and the friends of Nalle closing upon the officers, fearless and unterrified." [1]

After tearing Nalle away from the officers, the mob rushed to the waterfront, where "there was a skiff lying ready to start." Nalle was put on board, and an oarsman rowed across the river.

About four hundred of the rescuers followed by storming a Hudson River steam-powered ferry. It sailed immediately, carrying the rescuers, including Harriet, across the river to West Troy.

Nalle, still in handcuffs, darted off the boat as soon as it docked. But West Troy officers, probably alerted by telegraph, captured him again and hustled him into a room on the second floor of a building near the ferry dock. "The building was stoned," the *Daily Times* continued, "and the crowd, rushing up into the room under fire from the revolvers of the West Troy officers, seized the prisoner and escaped with him from the building. Nalle...was placed in a wagon and driven off..." Abolitionists hid him until they raised $650 to buy him from his owner. He then returned to Troy.

Harriet was not publicly identified at the time. She was about thirty-eight years old in 1860, so she disguised herself as an old lady. Was she acting as part of an escape she had planned in advance? She never said so, but the rescue skiff did arrive just when it was needed, and so did the wagon that carried Nalle off to a hiding place.

Whether or not the rescue was planned, its success gave Harriet a new triumph among sorrowing abolitionists who were mourning the hanging of John Brown—and singing "John Brown's body a lies a-mouldering in the grave." The abolitionists knew now that war was near and that it would soon shut down the Underground Railroad. Harriet decided to make one last trip to Maryland—where rumors that a slave revolt was brewing on the Eastern Shore were spreading fear among slave owners.

"WE MUST NOT BE ENEMIES," said Abraham Lincoln in his inaugural address on March 4, 1861. Behind him stands the unfinished Capitol.

Chapter 7.

Trouble in the Capital.

HARRIET'S LAST TRIP · LINCOLN IS ELECTED ·
SOUTH CAROLINA SECEDES · THE CONFEDERATE STATES
OF AMERICA IS FORMED · ASSASSINATION THREATS ·
UNION TROOPS REINFORCE FORT SUMTER

Harriet Tubman liked to lead Maryland slaves to freedom during the winter, when the nights were long and cold and when slave catchers rarely roamed the woods and marshes of Maryland's Eastern Shore. So she chose December 1860 for what was to be her last trip to lead slaves to freedom. It was a dangerous December, unlike any other she—or the nation— had ever known.

Maryland Governor Thomas Holliday Hicks feared that a slave revolt was brewing. Hicks knew the Eastern Shore very well, particularly

Harriet's home county of Dorchester, where he had been sheriff. Slave catchers were swarming in the area. "There is now much more risk on the road... than there has been for several months," one Underground Railroad conductor wrote to another.

December had become a time of great peril because of events following the November election of Abraham Lincoln. Governors in Southern states said that Lincoln could not be their President because he was against slavery.

South Carolina, the leading slave-owning state, seceded from the Union in December, and other states soon would do the same. "Civil war," said an Ohio newspaper, "is as certain to follow secession as darkness to follow the going down of the sun." Governor Hicks was refusing to call the Maryland legislature into session because he knew there would be a vote to take the state out of the Union. Hicks was trying to hold together a Border State— Southern in its traditions but Northern through its railroad, trade, and industrial connections. [1]

Harriet ignored the risks that awaited her in Maryland. In December 1860 she made her way

FIERY ANGER grips an anti-Lincoln crowd in Savannah, Georgia. Throughout the South, people saw the election of Lincoln as a reason to pull their states out of the Union. The first to leave was South Carolina.

to the Eastern Shore. As she later told a biographer, on that trip to Maryland she rescued seven people, including a crying baby. But was there another mission? Was she trying to find out whether Hicks was right about a possible slave revolt? All we know is that sometime around February 1861, Gerrit Smith, one of the Secret

Six, heard that slave catchers were looking for Harriet. He took her to Canada for her own safety. But she did not want to be safe. She wanted to get back to the United States, knowing that war was closer than ever.

By February 1861 six more states—Mississippi, Florida, Alabama, Georgia, Louisiana, and Texas—had seceded from the Union, joining South Carolina in what became a new nation, the Confederate States of America.

South Carolina demanded possession of all land held by the Federal government within the state's boundaries. The demand focused on three forts in Charleston harbor: Pinckney, manned by one sergeant; Moultrie, whose guns were aimed toward the sea; and Sumter, the only fort that could threaten Charleston. A thick-walled stronghold on an artificial island, Sumter commanded the entrance to the harbor. Major Robert Anderson was the highest-ranking Federal officer in the area. Expecting a Confederate attack, Anderson moved his troops from Fort Moultrie to Fort Sumter and waited for whatever the future would bring.

Lincoln began his presidency desperately hoping that he could preserve the Union, even though state after state was seceding over the issue of slavery. The president himself was in danger. He avoided an assassination attempt on the way to Washington to be sworn in. When he was inaugurated on March 4, 1861, soldiers who were sharpshooters stood on roofs near the Capitol. To stop anyone who might try to plant a bomb, soldiers were stationed under the platform where he took the oath of office. [2]

In his Inaugural Address, Lincoln reached out to the South, saying, "I have no purpose, directly or indirectly, to interfere with the institution of slavery in the states where it exists."

Lincoln knew that someday, somewhere, bullets would fly, and a war between North and South would begin. He had been President less than a month when he prepared for civil war by beginning a secret war in which no shots would be fired. It would be the war of spy versus spy, and it would draw Harriet Tubman into a new career.

A CONFEDERATE FLAG flies over Fort Sumter, a federal post that fell
to Southern conquerors in the opening act of the Civil War.

Chapter 8.

The Secret War.

LINCOLN'S SPYMASTER · HARRIET BUYS A HOUSE ·
FORT SUMTER FALLS · LINCOLN CALLS FOR VOLUNTEERS ·
BLOODY BALTIMORE · RUNAWAY GEORGE SCOTT
TEACHES GENERAL BUTLER A LESSON

Lincoln decided that he needed spies—and a trusted spymaster. He chose William H. Seward, the new Secretary of State. Lincoln knew that Seward, Harriet's longtime friend and benefactor, had been working for years as an abolitionist and Underground Railroad station master. And Lincoln knew that Harriet and other conductors would be valuable in the secret war. [1]

On April 2, Lincoln told Seward to pay $10,000 "from the secret service fund" to two Army officers to prepare an expedition to Fort Pickens, Florida. The expedition was so secret that neither the Secretary of War nor the Secretary of the Navy was told about it in advance. Nor did Lincoln tell Congress, whose members included many Confederate sympathizers, about what today would be called a "covert," or secret, operation.

Lincoln's concern about Fort Pickens showed that he realized that the Southern coast needed to be controlled by the Union. When war began, the South would depend upon getting supplies by sea. To seal Southern ports, the Union would use blockading warships—and spies.

Harriet Tubman and William Seward had met in the 1850s as fellow abolitionists. In 1857 Harriet had decided to move her parents, whom she had led out of Maryland slavery, from Canada to the United States. Seward, then governor of New York, offered her a two-story brick house that he owned in Auburn. He later sold her the house and its seven-acre site for $1,200 and arranged a mortgage. The sale was illegal at the time because the Supreme Court, in the Dred Scott decision of 1857,* ruled that slaves—even runaways in free

*See Note 7, Chapter 1.

A ROOFTOP AUDIENCE watches as Confederate guns in Charleston fire on the Union's Fort Sumter, the act that began the Civil War.

states—were not citizens and so had no rights, including the right to own property.

❀

At 4:30 a.m. on April 12, ten days after Lincoln began the secret war, a Confederate mortar on the Charleston shore fired a single shell. Its

MARCHING TO WAR, the 7th New York Militia parades down Broadway in April 1861, after Lincoln called for 75,000 volunteers to fight for the Union.

sputtering fuse traced half an arc across the starry sky. Then, in a flash of red and white light, the shell exploded directly over Fort Sumter. Responding to the signal, the shore guns roared. For thirty-four hours the shells fell on Fort Sumter, until it finally surrendered. Word of the bombardment and surrender spread through the North and South by telegraph. Beyond the last telegraph pole, the Pony Express carried the news westward: *WAR!* The next day, Lincoln asked the states still in the Union for 75,000 volunteers. [2]

The first to answer the call was Governor John A. Andrew of Massachusetts. A fiery abolitionist, Andrew had begun getting the militias ready as soon as he had become governor months before.

Andrew and other abolitionists in New England and New York knew that Harriet Tubman was an expert on Maryland's secret pathways. As an underground operative, she could provide the Union with a great deal of knowledge about Maryland, a Border State that was seesawing between the North and the South.

Andrew sent for Harriet at the beginning of the war, according to what she told an early biographer. Another, later biographer says she went to war with the troops of a second Massachusetts force, this one commanded by Brigadier General Benjamin F. Butler. [3]

Northern governors were part of the Union's military structure. They were like high-ranking officers without uniforms. They mobilized state regiments and commanded the men of their states when they were sent into battle. As the first governor to answer Lincoln's call, Andrew had great influence beyond the borders of Massachusetts. And Andrew, like Seward, joined Lincoln's secret war.

❊

The Massachusetts troops sent by Andrew left Boston for Washington on April 17. When they reached Baltimore, a pro-South mob was forming in the streets. The troops had to change trains, moving from one Baltimore station to another about a mile away. Horses pulled the rail cars to the second station because an old law restricted steam engines in the city. Some soldiers got through in the rail cars. But the mob blocked the rails, forcing the rest of the regiment to move across the city on foot. About 8,000 screaming, jeering people surrounded the soldiers.

The troops kept marching, even when many were struck by bricks and stones. Then men in the mob fired guns. Four soldiers fell. Their comrades fired back, killing about a dozen civilians. The first blood of the Civil War had been spilled.

BLOODY BALTIMORE. In Border State Maryland, a pro-South mob attacks Massachusetts troops heading for Washington in April 1861.

Lincoln and Seward now knew without a doubt that Maryland was full of Southern sympathizers.

The Massachusetts soldiers finally got to Washington by train. But Maryland officials destroyed railroad bridges to stop other Northern troops from reaching Washington via Baltimore. General Butler, leading another force out of Massachusetts, got as far as a destroyed bridge at Baltimore. That did not stop him. He took over a ferryboat, loaded his men aboard, and sailed for

Annapolis, where he expected to be able to board another train to Washington. Again Southern sympathizers tried to stop him, this time ripping up the rails around Annapolis.

Butler and a New York regiment, which had also arrived in Annapolis by ship, had expected to march on to the nation's capital along the Annapolis-Washington road. Instead, they decided to take the much more difficult route along the railroad tracks. A spy had warned that armed pro-South Marylanders were waiting to attack them on the Washington road. Who was the spy? We do not know.

Butler was promoted to major general and given command of a military district that included Virginia, North Carolina, and South Carolina. This meant that Andrew, as a powerful governor providing troops, would have great influence over that area.

Butler's headquarters was huge Fortress Monroe, at the eastern tip of the Virginia Peninsula, between the James and the York Rivers. Not long after the war began, a slave named George Scott escaped from a plantation near Yorktown and headed for freedom at Fortress Monroe. [4]

On the way to Monroe, Scott had noted two large Confederate fortifications. As soon as he reached Monroe, he told Union officers what he had seen. The officers, surprised at Scott's memory for details, still wondered if what he told them was true. He agreed to go back with an officer, who confirmed Scott's observations. Scott went back several times. On one trip, a Confederate sentinel spotted him and fired, putting a hole in Scott's jacket.

Scott's observations were the basis for Butler's attack on a Confederate position. Scott apparently was part of the attack force, for an official order says, "George Scott is to have a pistol." The attack ended in a Union defeat, which military historians blamed on military tactics, not the information that Scott provided.

Scott, as a runaway slave, accidentally took on the role of spy. He taught Butler, who had not been an abolitionist, an important lesson: *Fugitive slaves could be good spies.*

Soon after Butler took command of Fortress Monroe, three runaway slaves found their way there. They said they belonged to a slave owner

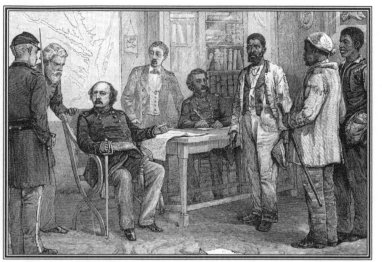

RUNAWAY SLAVES from Virginia plantations meet Major General Benjamin J. Butler at Fortress Monroe. He called them "contrabands," booty of war. Soon he learned their value as spies and scouts.

who was about to send them to work in North Carolina on Confederate fortifications.

Shortly after the three slaves arrived, a Virginia officer appeared under a flag of truce and demanded their return under the Fugitive Slave Act. Butler, famous back in Massachusetts as a shrewd lawyer, replied: "Virginia passed an ordinance of secession two days ago and claims to be a foreign country. I am under no constitutional obligations to a foreign country."

Butler said the ex-slaves were "contraband of war." By that rule of war, goods (contraband) that belong to the enemy can be seized.

Butler's decision created the term "contrabands" for fugitive slaves who sought freedom in Union Army camps. Throughout the official records of the war, there are frequent references to bits of intelligence coming from "contrabands." Many, for instance, as servants of Confederate officers, were able to report on battle-planning conversations that they had overheard.

Butler's discovery of the value of contrabands as spies was a turning point in the secret war. As for Harriet Tubman, Butler surely knew of her work, and, as a Massachusetts politician, he had to have known of the faith that Andrew, Seward, Gerrit Smith, and Higginson had in her. That faith now was extended to include other African Americans serving the Union as secret agents.

FLEEING TO FREEDOM, slaves—men, women, and children—arrive at
Fortress Monroe, where many began their missions as spies.

Chapter 9.

Black Dispatches.

Slave stampede · Contrabands as spies ·
Dabney's clothesline code · Richmond's lady spy ·
Mary Bowser and the Richmond White House ·
John Scobell's "Legal League"

So many "contrabands" made their way to Fortress Monroe that journalists called the flight "a slave stampede." Within a few weeks there were about 900 men, women, and children within the fortress. While President Lincoln and Congress struggled with the question of what to do with these self-freed slaves, General Butler began to use some of them as spies. Slaves uncovered information that only they could get. They had lived their lives as invisible people. That quality of invisibility, which Harriet Tubman knew so well, became the basis for using ex-slaves as spies for the Union.

One white spy even found that being a black slave was a good cover. She was Sarah Emma Edmonds, who enlisted in the Union Army as a man. Sometimes she put away her rifle and became a spy. To work in disguise, she blackened her face and hands and wandered behind the Confederate lines, observing fortifications and eavesdropping on conversations between officers. Confederate soldiers ignored her, seeing her as just another slave.

Union officers eventually got so many pieces of valuable information from slaves-turned-spies that intelligence officers put the reports in a special category: "Black Dispatches." The term is believed to have been first used by Colonel Rush Hawkins, a New Yorker commanding troops at Cape Hatteras, North Carolina. "If I want to find out anything hereabouts," he said, "I hunt up a Negro. And if he knows or can find out, I'm sure to get all I want."

Many slaves had been taken off plantations and ordered to work on Confederate fortifications. So, when they ran off to Union lines, they brought with them the best intelligence there is:

the kind that comes from a brave eyewitness. Many volunteered to work for the Union "within enemy lines," as official records described their mission. By using the cover of slave and going about their daily tasks while gathering information, they became what modern intelligence agencies call "stay-in-place agents." In a Union-occupied region of North Carolina, a report said about fifty volunteers "of the best and most courageous" ex-slaves were "kept constantly employed on the perilous but important duty of spies, scouts, and guides."

Spies went into Confederate territory to get whatever information they could find. Scouts, sent into enemy territory ahead of Union troops, got information of immediate use. Guides helped Union troops get from one point to another in unfamiliar territory.

Black spies did not need disguises or fake papers when they went on their missions. These "invaluable and almost indispensable" spies, as a Union official described them, depended on being looked upon as slaves, since most people in the South did not believe a slave was clever enough to be a spy. Black spies went as deep as 300 miles into Confederate territory, "bringing us back important and reliable information....They were pursued on several occasions by blood-hounds, two or three of them were taken prisoners; one of these was known to have been shot, and the fate of the others was not ascertained." Many a spying slave paid with his life before reaching Union territory.

Slaves ran what came to be called the "second Underground Railroad," which Union soldiers used to get to safety when they were trapped behind Confederate lines or when they escaped from Confederate prison camps. Slaves passed the soldiers from one cabin to another, from one safe place to the next.

Slaves who worked behind the lines needed a way to get their information speedily to Union officers. The use of clotheslines as signaling systems goes back at least to the Revolutionary War. That was the system that a Union officer said he saw near Fredericksburg, Virginia, when the Union and Confederate armies were on opposite sides of the Rappahannock River. A runaway slave named

CLOTHESLINE CODE. A slave spying for the Union sends a message about Confederate plans by hanging clothes in a certain way.

Dabney crossed into Union lines with his wife and, while doing odd jobs around the camp, got to learn the Union's wig-wag flag signaling system, which was used to send messages between signalers visible to each other.

After a while, Dabney's wife received permission to cross the river to work as a spying house slave. Soon Dabney started reporting accurate intelligence about Confederate plans to Union officers. When asked how he managed to gather the intelligence, he told about the signaling system that he and his wife used. On her side of the river, a clothesline hung near a cabin within sight of the Union camp across the river. The couple's code was based on what was hung and where it was hung. A white shirt represented a certain Confederate general, and a pair of pants hung upside down indicated that the general was taking troops westward. The clothesline signaling continued until the Union camp moved elsewhere and the Dabneys moved into spying legend.

Richmond, Virginia, the Confederacy's capital city, was the main target for Union intelligence-gathering. It was also the home of Elizabeth Van Lew, Southern socialite and Union spy.

Elizabeth Van Lew grew up in an elegant Richmond mansion. Her family owned slaves who worked in the mansion and on a family farm outside the city. As a woman in prewar Richmond, she should have been part of the city's social elite. But when her father died, she freed her slaves, a gesture that shocked and surprised her neighbors. There was gossip about her anti-slavery beliefs.

SPY HEADQUARTERS. Elizabeth Van Lew's Richmond home hid a major spy. Van Lew ran agents who gathered information that she sent to Union officers outside the Confederate capital city.

She first showed her sympathy for the despised Union by caring for Yankee prisoners of war held in Richmond prisons. She charmed one prison keeper, Lieutenant David H. Todd (half-brother of Mary Todd Lincoln, the President's wife), by bringing him gingerbread and butter-milk. Neither he nor any other official realized that slaves inside the prison gathered information for her. She and they were members of a spy ring that provided the Union with a steady flow of intelligence out of the Confederate capital.

Another African American in Elizabeth's ring was William Brisby, a free black who worked as a blacksmith and fisherman. He had Confederate Army passes that let him enter and leave Richmond to fish, get supplies, and sell his catch. He managed to shepherd about one hundred escaped prisoners and runaway slaves out of the city by hiding them under loads he carried in his horse-drawn cart. Once he was arrested by suspicious officials. But they let him go because, luckily, he had not yet picked up his secret passengers, and the Confederates could not prove he was a spy. When he was released, he went on smuggling people.

Elizabeth Van Lew learned to outwit Confederate spy hunters by using techniques that modern intelligence officers would recognize. She used "drops"—secret hiding places—to pass secret messages and sent "cutouts" to meetings so that she would avoid direct contact with agents.

General Butler, at Fortress Monroe, first learned about Van Lew and her "Richmond Underground" from the escape stories told by two Union soldiers. Butler, needing a dependable spymaster, sent one of the escapees back to the Confederate capital, where he contacted Van Lew. He gave her a simple cipher system to use for her reports to Butler. She kept the key to the cipher in the case of her watch (see page 172).

She sometimes wrote her coded messages on small pieces of paper, rolled them into balls, and gave each to a separate courier. In this way, if a courier were caught, all that would be found would be a scrap of paper with numbers written on it.

CONFEDERATE CIPHER wheel used a letter substitution system for secret messages.

She also used a cutout in her own home to begin the journey of a message from Richmond to Fortress Monroe. She would place the message under one of the two small sculptures of lions that crouched on either side of the fireplace in her library. Later, the cutout—an old black servant—

A SECRET MESSAGE, written in code by spymaster Elizabeth Van Lew, is taken from a fireplace "drop" in her home by one of her servant spies.

would go into the library and, while appearing to dust the fireplace, pick up the enciphered message. Next, he would go to the Van Lew farm, just outside Richmond. To anyone watching him, he looked like just another slave doing a chore. At the farm, another courier would take the message on the next leg of its journey.

Butler was so pleased with the information he received "from a lady in Richmond" that he sent a sample to Secretary of War Edwin M. Stanton.

In it, Van Lew told where new artillery batteries were being set up, reported that three cavalry regiments had been "disbanded by General Lee for want of horses" and that "It is intended to remove to Georgia very soon all the Federal prisoners." [1]

In June 1864, Union General Ulysses S. Grant attacked Petersburg, south of Richmond. Unable to take Petersburg, Grant settled in for what would become a nine-month siege. When the siege began, Grant's brilliant intelligence officer, Colonel George H. Sharpe, took over Elizabeth Van Lew and her ring from Butler. Sharpe set up five "depots," where couriers, mostly black agents, could deliver their reports.

By the time Elizabeth began serving Sharpe, she had more than a dozen agents and couriers, including her own African-American servants. Sometimes they hid messages among the paper patterns in a seamstress's belongings or carried messages in scraped-out eggs placed among whole eggs. Another agent was a baker who used his delivery wagon as a cover for picking up reports and passing them along.

Much of what Van Lew reported to Sharpe is unknown, but after the war he wrote that the "greater portion of our intelligence in 1864–65" came from her and the white and black members of her ring. Not one of the black agents was ever caught, and most remain unknown to this day.

One of her black spies, however, does have a name—a name that may not be her real name. Like all great spies, Mary Elizabeth Bowser left behind more questions than answers. But the clues are many and the evidence is strong that she was the boldest spy of the war. She is believed to have worked as a servant in the mansion of Confederate President Jefferson Davis. The Richmond White House, as the mansion was called, was Davis's official residence and office.

A house slave would have overheard conversations between Davis and high-ranking officers and officials. And she would have seen papers on Davis's desk. No one would notice her. After all, she was a young female slave who could not read or write. Nor would anyone look twice at a slave running an errand. Nor would anyone believe that the errand was to a farm not only to pick up vegetables but also to put a message in a drop run by the Van Lew spy ring.

❀

The story of Mary, the Richmond White House spy, begins in 1846 when a Van Lew slave named Mary Jane Richards was baptized in St. John's Episcopal Church. Attended by Richmond's wealthiest whites, the church was revered as the site where Patrick Henry said, "Give me liberty or give me death." Richmond social leaders were shocked, but they were used to Elizabeth Van Lew's strange ways. Later, Van Lew sent Mary Jane off to Philadelphia for an education and then to Liberia, the African nation founded by Americans as a colony for ex-slaves. [2]

After working in Liberia as a missionary, Mary Jane Richards went back to Richmond in 1860—an illegal act for a freed slave under a Virginia law that punished returning freed slaves by re-enslaving them. The Van Lew family paid a $10 fine but claimed that Mary Jane was still a slave. This statement would give her perfect cover as an agent.

In April 1861, Mary Jane Richards was married in Richmond to Wilson Bowser, possibly a free black. And, with a slight, unexplained change in name—Mary *Elizabeth* Bowser—she enters spy history. Sometime later, she is said to have gone to work as a house slave for Jefferson Davis.

This is not as peculiar as it sounds. Davis, who was from Mississippi, first served as President in the original Confederate capital in Montgomery, Alabama. When Richmond was made the capital city in July 1861, he was installed in one of its mansions. He and his wife would have relied upon local people to suggest house slaves. People in Richmond were well aware of Elizabeth Van Lew's pro-Union sympathies. Members of her ring, however, lived the double lives of prominent citizen and spy while appearing to be typical Southerners. (They included merchants, a railroad official, and an unsuccessful candidate for mayor of Richmond.) One of them could have suggested that Mary (perhaps using another name) be taken on as a servant.

Thomas McNiven, who worked in a bakery and who claimed that he was part of the Richmond

Underground, later said that Elizabeth's "colored girl, Mary, was the best" [spy] because she was working in the Davis home and "had a photographic mind." He went on to say, "Everything she saw on the Rebel President's desk she could repeat word for word.... She made a point of always coming out to my wagon when I made deliveries at the Davis home to drop information." [3]

SPYING SLAVE Mary Bowser looks through President Jefferson Davis's papers.

The Davis office-home was not very well protected. Unknown slaves tried once to burn it down. William A. Jackson, a slave who worked for President Davis as a coachman, was more successful. He slipped out of the house, made it to Union lines, and provided Major General Irvin McDowell with information about the plans of various Confederate generals and their reaction to Union tactics. Major McDowell telegraphed some of Jackson's reports directly to Secretary of War Edwin M. Stanton:

"He reports scraps of conversation overheard by him while driving Mr. and Mrs. Davis in the carriage and between Mr. Davis and those who came to see him....The coachman represents that Mrs. Davis said the Confederacy was about played out...that there is much outspoken Union feeling in Richmond."

Like William Jackson, John Scobell did his best work by listening. Scobell specialized in getting information from slaves as he traveled around the Confederacy, posing as a cook, a food vendor, or a laborer. He was taking advantage of the fact that Confederate officials allowed slaves to journey from the plantations where they lived to places where war work was needed. So a slave who was a stranger was not an oddity in the wartime South.

Scobell used his membership in the "Legal League" to relay information. This was a secret black organization whose members spied for the Union and aided runaway slaves and escaped Union prisoners. As a member, Scobell knew the ritual:

You rap on the door of the cabin and someone within asks, "Who comes?"

You answer: "Friends of Uncle Abe."

"What do you desire?"

"Light and loyalty."

If Scobell discovered urgent intelligence—such as the size and location of Confederate supply depots—he would ask league members to take the information to Union forces. He would then travel on, seeking secrets and passing them on, just as so many African Americans were doing. We do not know their names. But we know what General Robert E. Lee, commander of the Confederate Army of Northern Virginia, had to say about the men and women of the Black Dispatches: "The chief source of information to the enemy is through our Negroes."

RUNNING THE UNION BLOCKADE, a Confederate paddlewheel steamer
nears her goal—Wilmington, North Carolina.

Chapter 10.

Black Spies and the Anaconda Plan.

BLOCKADING THE SOUTH · MARY TOUVESTRE'S
SURPRISING REPORT · ROBERT SMALLS AND THE *PLANTER* ·
THE STORMING OF PORT ROYAL BAY · MAJOR HUNTER
BECOMES A HERO · HARRIET GOES TO HILTON HEAD

Soon after the war began, U.S. Navy warships started steaming along coasts from Virginia to Texas, trying to keep ships from entering or leaving Southern ports. The Confederates sent out their own warships to break the naval blockade, as such an operation is called. Also sailing to aid the South were privateers, daring private ship owners and captains whose ships carried cargoes of guns, ammunition, and other supplies, mostly from British ports. The North's blockade was named the Anaconda Plan, after the snake that slowly strangles its prey.

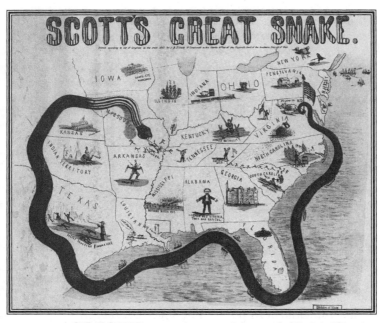

A GREAT SNAKE squeezes the coasts and threatens the Mississippi River in this cartoon of Union General Winfield Scott's Anaconda Plan.

The Anaconda Plan did more than send Union ships to Southern coasts. The plan became part of a war-winning Union strategy that drew Harriet Tubman to South Carolina as a secret agent. It also gave many other African Americans in the South a chance to work for the North.

One important Southern port was Norfolk, Virginia, a key naval and shipbuilding center. Mary Touvestre, a freed slave, was a housekeeper in Norfolk. Her employer was an engineer who was working on an important project at the Norfolk Navy Yard. [1]

When Virginia seceded, Union forces had fled from Norfolk after setting fire to the Navy Yard and several ships, including one called the *Merrimack*, which burned to the waterline and sank. Confederates raised the ship, renamed her *Virginia*, and started repairing her in secrecy.

That was the project that Mary Touvestre heard the engineer mention to his fellow workers. They talked when she was around because they considered her too ignorant to be able to understand what they were saying to each other.

But Mary realized that the men were building a new kind of ship—an ironclad warship that could destroy the wooden-hulled Union blockaders. Union cannonballs would bounce off *Virginia's* iron sides, which were one to four inches thick. The *Virginia* also had an iron prow with an underwater ram designed to slam into and splinter the side of an enemy ship.

One day, the engineer brought home a set of plans. When Mary was alone, she stole the plans, hid them in her dress, and headed north to Washington. She carried a paper showing that she was a freed slave. But, at best, that would only get her to Confederate lines. She would have to risk her life to keep traveling on to Washington because word was spreading through the Confederacy that slaves were no longer to be trusted.

When Mary arrived in Washington, she managed to meet with Gideon Welles, Lincoln's Secretary of the Navy. In his office, he later wrote, she reported that "the ship was nearly finished, had come out of the dock, and was about receiving her armament." To prove her story, she handed Welles the plans and other documents she had carried from Norfolk.

Welles, surprised by Mary's report, speeded up the building of the Union's own ironclad, the *Monitor.* Before the *Monitor* could reach Norfolk, the *Virginia* sank two Union blockade ships and

IRONCLADS CLASH in an historic duel between the Union *Monitor* (left) and the Confederate *Virginia* off Hampton Roads, Virginia. Neither won the fight, which ended the age of wooden warships.

damaged a third. But the *Monitor* arrived in time to attack the *Virginia*. [2]

If Mary Touvestre had not told Welles about the *Virginia*, a historian wrote, "the *Virginia* could have had several more unchallenged weeks to destroy Union ships—setting back the Anaconda Plan by opening Norfolk to blockade runners that were carrying urgently needed supplies."

Like Mary Touvestre, Robert Smalls saw a chance to help the Union. Born a slave in Beaufort,

South Carolina, he had been hired out by his master to ships that constantly sailed in and out of the South's busiest harbor, Charleston, South Carolina. When the war started, Smalls was put on board the *Planter*, a small steamship that carried ammunition and other supplies to Confederate gun batteries in Charleston. The ship also served as a water taxi for the Confederate commander in Charleston. As the *Planter's* pilot, Smalls learned to navigate through the waters of the complex port, adding to his knowledge about the coast from Beaufort to Florida.

One night, the ship's officers went ashore to attend a party, leaving the slave crew in possession of the ship. Smalls smuggled his wife and family on board, along with relatives of the black crew. He then put on the captain's uniform and broad-brimmed straw hat and took over the ship. From the pilot house he steered the ship past the forts that guarded the harbor, sounding the correct whistle signal for each fort.

Cleared for passage out of the harbor, he steamed beyond the range of Charleston's shore guns and then headed toward the nearest Union blockade ship, the U.S.S. *Onward.* Her guns were bearing on the *Planter* when Smalls raised a white flag and came alongside. He raised his hat and shouted to a surprised Union officer: "Good morning, sir!"

Rear Admiral Samuel F. Dupont, commander of the South Atlantic Blockading Squadron, listened eagerly as Smalls told what he knew about Confederate coastal defenses, especially in and around Charleston. Dupont accepted the *Planter* into the U. S. Navy and kept Smalls as her pilot.

On November 7, 1861, Dupont tightened the Anaconda Plan's stranglehold on the South Carolina coast when he led the largest fleet the U. S. Navy had ever sent to sea—77 ships, including transports carrying more than 12,000 troops—into Port Royal Bay and began bombarding Confederate forts. "The noise was terrific, while bursting of the shells was terrible as it was destructive," a *New York Herald* correspondent wrote about the naval barrage. "I counted no less than forty shells bursting at one time." [3]

SLAVES NO MORE, hundreds of black Americans accompany Union troops as they advance into Southern territory. Thousands of ex-slaves went on to aid the Union as soldiers or spies.

Sounds of the explosions were heard for miles up and down the coast, setting off a panicky flight of plantation owners and their families. They left behind thousands of slaves, who flocked to Union encampments.

On December 11, Union troops landed on Port Royal, one of the offshore barrier islands, so called because they protect the low-lying, marshy shore during storms. Port Royal Island, about midway between Savannah, Georgia, and Charleston, gave the Union a key location for attacks on either city. Union troops occupied Port Royal Island's two towns, Port Royal and Beaufort, along with dozens of nearby islands, including Hilton Head Island and Parris Island.

White families fled from the invaders while slaves, in the words of a Union soldier, "came flocking into our camp by the hundreds...many of them with no other clothing than gunny-sacks." They arrived, said a Union report, "carrying in little bundles, all their worldly possessions, having a simple faith that when they reached 'Massa Lincum's soldiers' they would be free."

The Union had hoped to take Charleston, but the city successfully fought off invasion. Dupont blockaded Charleston while focusing on the basic Union strategy: occupy or isolate South Carolina, Georgia, and Florida, not only cutting them off from the rest of the Confederacy but also getting their ports into Union hands.

Dupont got valuable information from runaway slaves like Small. The admiral ordered his officers to pay attention to what the contrabands had to say because they knew the Carolina and Georgia coasts, a maze of jagged shoreline and numerous islands. They also knew the rivers that served as roads for transporting rice and indigo from riverside plantations.

The contrabands also helped guide Union sailors along coasts where Confederates had destroyed lighthouses and channel markers. Slaves told captains about the peculiarities of sandbars, tides, and currents. Those who had put mines or obstacles in rivers either guided Union ships around them or removed them. As a result, Union forces eventually spread their hold on the river-laced coast as far as northern Florida.

Admiral Dupont's reports on the work and courage of Robert Smalls and the contrabands led Navy Secretary Welles to approve the enlistment of former slaves. More than 1,000 men who had been enslaved in South Carolina, Georgia, and Florida joined the Blockading Squadron. [4]

In the spring of 1862 Union forces destroyed Fort Pulaski, which guarded Savannah. That victory,

SECRET WEAPON. Confederates plant a cylinder-shaped "torpedo" (mine) in the harbor of Charleston, South Carolina. Confederate mines sank at least thirty-seven Union ships and damaged many more.

which cut Savannah off from the sea, made a hero of Major General David Hunter. He became commander of the Union Army's Department of the South, which included Georgia, Florida, and South Carolina. Hunter immediately declared that all the slaves in the states he controlled were "forever free."

In Boston, Governor Andrew was keeping a close watch on how ex-slaves in South Carolina had begun serving the Union. He had excellent sources through his contacts with Secretary of State Seward and others involved in spy activities. Andrew also knew that the enlisting of ex-slaves by Navy Secretary Welles and the freeing of slaves by General Hunter had challenged President Lincoln.

The President, who personally hated slavery, had been telling passionate abolitionists like Andrew that, above all, he wanted to "save the Union," even if that meant not pleasing the abolitionists with a declaration ending slavery. Lincoln had unsuccessfully tried to solve the problem by recommending to Congress that ex-slaves who fled to Union camps be sent to colonies in Haiti or Central America at government expense.

Andrew and many other Northern abolitionists wanted Lincoln to give official freedom to the thousands of ex-slaves who had gone over to Union lines, ending their vague "contraband" status. That change could be started by having Congress wipe out the 1792 law that prohibited the enlistment of "persons of color" in the army.

As Frederick Douglass wrote: "Once let the black man get upon his person the brass letters U.S., let him get an eagle on his button, and a musket on his shoulder and bullets in his pocket, and there is no power on earth that can deny him that he has earned the right to citizenship."

President Lincoln had fired Major General John C. Frémont for ordering the freeing of slaves in his command. This action enraged abolitionists, including Harriet who said that God would not let Lincoln beat the South until he did "the right thing." Although Lincoln didn't fire Hunter, he did cancel the general's "forever free" decree. Now, Andrew decided, was the right time to do the right thing. [5]

One of Harriet's friends later wrote: "Harriet Tubman was sent to Hilton Head—she says—in May 1862, at the suggestion of Governor Andrew, with the idea that she would be a valuable person to operate within the enemies' lines—in procuring information & scouts." Her cover story was that she was going to Beaufort as a volunteer for the New England Freedman's Aid Society.

A CONFEDERATE TORPEDO explodes under the *Commodore Barney*, damaging, but not sinking, the Union warship.

Chapter 11.

Harriet Goes to War.

QUEEN OF THE CAROLINA SEA ISLANDS · THE HARD LIFE
OF BEAUFORT SLAVES · HARRIET'S GULLAH RECRUITS ·
HUNTING TORPEDOES · UNDERCOVER HARRIET ·
THE EMANCIPATION PROCLAMATION

Beaufort called itself the Queen of the Carolina Sea Islands. The little port town had grown rich on the crops of South Carolina's stretch of flatlands and marshes known as the Lowcountry. That fertile coast and its nearby Sea Islands made a relatively few white families wealthy by producing millions of tons of rice and Sea Island cotton, which was known for its long, silky strands.

A local historian called Beaufort "the most cultured town of its size in America," a place where wealthy planters spent their time attending parties, hunting, fishing, racing their sailboats, and enjoying a life of leisure, while, back on the plantations, overseers put thousands of slaves to work from dawn to dusk.

"If you ask me what I am doing, I should tell you 'nothing,'" Edward Barnwell Heyward wrote to a friend in 1855. "My father is a Rice planter and his Sons have enough money to live handsomely and at leisure."

Each year, at the end of May, out of fear of getting malaria—called "country fever"—the white families moved away from their plantations and did not return until the first week in November. Most planters spent the time with relatives or friends in other parts of South Carolina or in other states. Some went to Europe.

Slaves were left behind on the plantation, under the control of overseers. Day after day, under sun and in rain, they dug and maintained the mazes of ditches and drains needed to control the flow of water through the rice fields. Rice slaves were worked harder and had tougher lives than most slaves elsewhere.

An overseer on a rice plantation told how he managed two
slaves bought in Maryland:
"They were running away
every day. I gave them a hundred lashes more than a dozen
times. But they never quit running away, 'til I chained them
together, with iron collars
round their necks, and chained
them to spades, and made them
do nothing but dig ditches...."

RICE HARVESTERS smash rice,
husking grains with heavy pestles. Slaves
hid rice in aprons to feed their families.

Cotton harvest came
when the humid summer days
were long and steamy. The
precious cotton was usually put in bags, rather
than baled, to protect the delicate strands.
Sometimes slaves had to remove cotton seeds by
hand instead of running the cotton through the
teeth of a cotton gin, which was the way that
tougher upland cotton was treated.

Each slave was expected to pick a hundred
pounds of cotton a day. This was an immense

COTTON SLAVES—men, women, and children—worked from dawn to dusk. On South Carolina plantations, each slave was expected to pick one hundred pounds of cotton each day. Owners called their slaves "movable property."

amount, considering that every tuft of cotton had to be pulled from its pod. The men, women, and children did not have shoes. Many were bitten by snakes or by caterpillars called "stinging worms." Slaves who failed to pick a hundred pounds risked flogging. Overseers wielded rawhide whips and wooden paddles riddled with holes designed to raise blisters on bared backs.

"During the cotton-picking season," a runaway slave remembered, "the place was filled with screams of agony every evening."

South Carolina's slaves needed no convincing when asked if they wanted to fight for the Union.

✹

When Harriet arrived in Beaufort, she quickly turned to recruiting the ex-slaves pouring into Union camps in Beaufort and Hilton Head. Many of her recruits were from the Lowcountry and the Sea Islands. They spoke what white people called Gullah, perhaps from the word "Angola," one of the West African countries the slaves came from.

Gullah mixes English words (including some from Shakespeare's time) with grammar and pronunciations from its African roots. Unlike most American slaves, Lowcountry slaves lived apart from and had little contact with whites, including their often-absent masters. Thus, their language developed independently.

"They laughed when they heard me talk, and I could not understand them, no how," Harriet later remembered. Speaking about a funeral she attended in the Lowcountry, she told of sweet voices, singing "everything we sing," along with "a great many hymns that we can't never catch at all."

Harriet may have heard someone point to another person and say, *troot ma-wt*, meaning "truth mouth," a truthful person. Or she might have been warned about a robber by being told *i han shaht pay-shun*, meaning "His hand is short of patience"—a polite way of saying, "He steals." Passing a cemetery, a Gullah speaker might say *sho ded*, meaning "sho [surely] dead," the Gullah expression for cemetery. Union soldiers were "Yankee Buckra," a Gullah version of Confederate slang, "Yankee bucks." [1]

Harriet convinced many of the male ex-slaves that the Yankee Buckras were good men who were fighting to end slavery. And she helped the black families by setting up a laundry, where women earned money washing clothes for the white soldiers. She also taught them to sew and bake for the Yankee dollar.

The ex-slaves shared what one white observer called a mysterious communication, meaning that they kept information among themselves and shut out their overseers. Harriet tapped into this communication system as she gradually won their trust and began to recruit some of the men as spies, scouts, and pilots. [2]

The pilots knew the rivers because they had worked on boats used for carrying rice and cotton from riverside plantations to ports. Pilots helped Union naval officers make their way up rivers, keeping them away from shallows and warning them of Confederate "torpedoes," as river and sea mines were called then.

Typically, a river torpedo was a sunken five-gallon jug or a barrel filled with gunpowder and anchored just beneath the surface. Two insulated wires ran from the torpedo to the shore, where a hidden Confederate soldier waited. When a Union ship passed over the jug, the soldier hit a plunger on a battery device, creating a spark that set off the gunpowder. Other, larger, more complicated torpedoes were used to defend Charleston and other Southern harbors. One model was designed to explode when struck by a

HIDDEN HAZARDS under the surface of a river, Confederate mines await Union ships. Hands grasp wires connecting mines to battery-operated devices. Switched on, they explode mines as ships pass over.

ship's hull. The explosion was triggered when a thin lead tube was crushed, breaking a glass vial inside. Sulphuric acid spilled out, mixing with other chemicals to produce a small explosion that set off about fifty pounds of gunpowder. [3]

While Harriet recruited spies and soldiers, she also worked at various tasks in Beaufort and Hilton Head. She later gave several accounts of her war days. Piecing the accounts together, we get a picture of a woman of many skills. She could serve as a nurse in a hospital, bathing soldiers'

ON A DANGEROUS MISSION, Union sailors load a Confederate mine into their boat. A wrong move could explode the mine, killing all. Black spies often spotted mines and helped Union teams remove them.

wounds or holding down a man who was having a leg amputated without anesthesia. She could wade into a marsh, pull up some roots, add them to herbs, and produce a medicine. At a Union camp where soldiers were "dying off like sheep" from dysentery, she "dug some roots and herbs and made a tea...and it cured them." She could also bake and sell pies and gingerbread to earn the money needed to care for black men, women, and children.

Harriet did the work that had to be done. But most of all she wanted to go to war, and two men who arrived in South Carolina would help take her there: Thomas Wentworth Higginson, Harriet's old Massachusetts friend, and James Montgomery, who had ridden with John Brown against slaveholders in "Bloody Kansas."

The recruitment of ex-slaves, begun by General Hunter and continued by Harriet, produced the First South Carolina Volunteers, made up of ex-slave soldiers with white officers.[*] As the regiment was taking shape, sixty-two of its men went off to raid Confederate outposts along the Georgia-Florida coast. The leading sergeant on the raid had been the most valuable slave on a nearby plantation. He volunteered even though he knew that for his capture a slave catcher could get a $2,000 reward—an enormous sum at the time.

The raiders brought back large amounts of rice and lumber, along with 155 slaves, 94 of whom enlisted in the regiment. That was the first proof to any doubters that black soldiers could fight and could inspire others to join and fight.

[*]In February 1864 the regiment's name was changed to the Thirty-third United States Colored Infantry.

When the regiment of nearly 800 men was officially formed in November 1862, Higginson, who had been sent to South Carolina by Governor Andrew, became its commanding officer. Higginson, Montgomery, and Harriet now found themselves carrying out, in the Deep South, the plan that John Brown had conceived for the Appalachian Mountains: Find slaves, arm them, and send them against the slaveholders until, with more and more ex-slaves armed, the slaveholders would be defeated.

On January 1, 1863, abolitionists received the help from Lincoln that they had been hoping for: his Emancipation Proclamation, which declared that all slaves in Confederate-controlled areas were "forever free." Though the proclamation didn't liberate the slaves in the Border States, it encouraged slaves in the South to flee across Union lines. The loss of so many workers further weakened the Confederacy.

Twenty-two days after the Emancipation Proclamation, Higginson's men, who had freed themselves before Lincoln did, went off to war.

INVADING THE SOUTH, Union soldiers and warships joined in amphibious operations along sea and river shores from North Carolina to Florida.

Chapter 12.

The General
Leads a Raid.

BATTLE ON THE ST. MARYS RIVER · HARRIET PLANS A
RAID · "FREEDOM SHIPS" ON THE COMBAHEE ·
THE BATTLE FOR CHARLESTON · PRAISE FOR HARRIET
AND THE BLACK DISPATCHES

Colonel Higginson and his men fought their first battle along the St. Marys River, which flows out of the great Okefenokee swamp, forming the southeastern boundary between Georgia and Florida. Decaying vegetation stained the water a glassy black so that the moon shimmered on the St. Marys as Higginson and 462 men set out in three warships.

This was a covert operation, a guerrilla raid into Confederate territory to seize lumber and other supplies for Union camps. The three ships, each armed with cannon, were the *Ben De Ford,* a steamer that carried Higginson and most of the men; the *John Adams*, an old Boston ferry-boat converted to a warship; and the *Planter*, the ex-Confederate ship that Robert Smalls had delivered to the Union. [1]

Higginson, a former minister who had little military experience but a big hatred for slavery, was enthusiastic about leading the raid. "I always thought a pirate's life must be fascinating," he later wrote in his journal, adding, "& so it is."

Before setting out, Higginson had huddled with black spies and jotted in a notebook many bits of intelligence about "vulnerable points along the coast, charts of rivers, locations of pickets [Confederate sentinels]." Spies who had worked in the pine forests along the river told him about a riverside lumberyard stacked high with boards. That was the most important objective of the raid.

Just after midnight, fifteen miles up the river, Higginson and about a hundred men went ashore. They hiked silently along a path that had been hacked out of the piney woods by lumber slaves. The corporal now leading Higginson had been one of those slaves. The corporal captured a slave lingering near the path who was suspicious of these armed black soldiers until he was shown a copy of the Emancipation Proclamation and told its meaning. "Governor Andrew had sent me a large printed supply," Higginson later wrote. "We seldom found men who could read it, but they all seemed to feel more secure when they held it in their hands."

FREEDOM finally came to slaves in the form of President Lincoln's 1863 Emancipation Proclamation.

As the men made their way along the path, Confederate soldiers attacked the advance guard. Both sides fired into the darkness. In the short, deafening exchange of fire, twelve Confederates were killed, along with one black soldier, shot in the heart. Seven black soldiers were wounded. One would later die. Another, shot in the shoulder, asked a comrade to dig out the buckshot so he would not have to go off duty to get medical aid.

RIVER RAID by Colonel Higginson and his black and white troops ends with
men carrying off food for Union soldiers and plantation property, including a
piano that was later given to a school for ex-slaves.

The mission continued. The men found the
house where the Confederate pickets had stayed.
The raiders burned the house to the ground,
after removing a piano, which was later carried
back to a ship. The piano was given to a school in
Beaufort, where white abolitionists from New
England were teaching ex-slaves to read and write.

Farther upriver, the ships reached a wharf. The
men silently filed off the ships, surrounded a cluster
of buildings, captured a few prisoners, and seized

the lumber mill and the home of the owner. Shocked by the sudden appearance of the raiders, the owner was even more shocked to meet a corporal ushered into her house by Higginson. The corporal had been one of her slaves.

The corporal quietly led Higginson to a small building called "the slave jail." Inside were three stocks—hinged boards notched to form holes for the neck, hands, and feet. Slaves had been locked into the stocks for punishment. One stock with small holes was used to lock up women and children.

At various stops upriver, the raiders collected lumber, bricks, railroad rails, and other cargo, along with several slave families and a new scout, who provided "much valuable information." On the voyage downstream, Confederate soldiers on high bluffs fired down on the raiders, killing the captain of Higginson's ship. The black soldiers fired back, shouting to each other, "Never give it up!" Their gunfire and the ship's cannon silenced the Confederates.

Back in camp, his nine-day expedition finished, Higginson presented to General Hunter the stocks and shackles from the slave jail. In his report to Hunter, Higginson said, "No officer in this regiment now doubts that the key to the successful prosecution of this war lies in the unlimited employment of black troops. Their superiority lies simply in the fact that they know the country, while white troops do not....It would have been madness to attempt, with the bravest white troops, what I have successfully accomplished with black ones...." [2]

Harriet and other recruiters, meanwhile, had enlisted enough ex-slaves to create the Second Regiment of South Carolina. The commanding officer would be Colonel James Montgomery.

He and Higginson had very different views about the way to fight a war. Higginson made sure that his men understood the difference between looting and taking what the Union Army needed. (He believed that the piano he had taken was not loot because it was going to a black school. And he approved of taking a few sheep and cows now and then because food was needed by the Union.)

Montgomery said he could order the burning of civilian property when he believed it was necessary for winning the war. He had been known in prewar Kansas as a jayhawker, which meant a wild, vengeful guerrilla. He believed in burning and looting. Black Union soldiers, he said, "are outlawed, and therefore not bound by the rules of regular warfare." As for Southerners, they "were to be swept away by the hand of God." [3]

Around this time, General Hunter, who was well aware of Harriet's work as a spy and recruiter of spies in the rivers and marshes of his command, asked her if she would go on a river raid. A general usually doesn't ask; he gives orders. But Harriet had an odd role. Although she was a civilian, she was also attached to the Union Army. She was a woman, and so in those days she was doing what women were expected to do: cook or work in a hospital. But, as a scout and spy, she was doing what male soldiers did. And she had the power to spend "secret service" funds, enabling her to work secretly on her own, outside the army chain of command.

Hunter told her that the raid would be along the Combahee River, dangerous because of torpedoes.

They would have to be found and removed. Then the raiders were to go far up the river, destroying bridges, rescuing slaves, and doing as much damage as possible to the riverside plantations. The raid was a key part of the Union plan to strike hard at the South's rice crops, which provided food to Confederates and wealth to South Carolina.

Harriet boldly told Hunter that she would go only if Colonel James Montgomery commanded the operation. Hunter agreed, and Harriet and Montgomery began planning the raid.

The Combahee—pronounced *Chumbee*—was a long, twisting river, so narrow in places that the trees formed a green arch, blocking out much of the sky. It was a place of eagles and osprey, alligators and snakes. Mosquitoes were so thick that if you wiped them off your arm, your hand was black with them. Cattails and the knobby roots of cypress lined the jagged shores of the lower Combahee. Then came the briar-covered dikes of miles and miles of riverbank rice plantations. [4]

A raid along the Combahee would strike at the heart of South Carolina's old and fabulously

THE JAGGED COASTLINE of South Carolina became a battlefield for the Union Army and Navy. Plantations lined rivers, highways to the sea for rice and cotton. This map shows the area of Harriet's raid.

wealthy slaveholder society. The largest plantations along the river and its tributaries belonged to the Heyward family, which settled in the area early in the 17th century. Thomas Heyward, Jr., was a signer of the Declaration of Independence.

When his descendent, Nathaniel Heyward, died in 1851, he had 1,829 slaves—more than any other slaveholder in the United States. By the time the Civil War started, the Heyward family owned about 3,000 slaves. One family member was Edward Barnwell Heyward, the man who had boasted that as a rich and idle rice grower he could live "handsomely and at leisure."

❋

Harriet took over the planning of the raid, basing her strategy on what her agents had learned about Confederate defenses along the river and the torpedoes that were in it. She knew the area fairly well by now, thanks to her own observations and the reports she received from her scouts.

Some of the intelligence came to her because she was known and trusted by men and women in Confederate territory who knew bits of information, such as the fact that Confederate pickets had pulled out of Tar Bluff, downriver from Combahee Ferry.

Montgomery handled the military strategy, combining standard army tactics with the guerrilla warfare he had learned long ago in Kansas. Although he was in charge as the commanding officer, Harriet was the real leader of the black soldiers. She had recruited many of them and had helped their families.

In the predawn of June 1, 1863, about three hundred of those men went aboard the gunboats *Harriet A. Weed, Sentinel,* and *John Adams.* Gunners from the Third Rhode Island Battery set up extra cannon on the deck of the *Adams.*

"When we went up the river in the morning," Harriet later said, recalling that June day, "it was just about light. The fog was rising over the rice fields, and the people was just done with their breakfast and was going out to the field." Harriet and Montgomery were on the deck of the lead ship, the *John Adams,* whose pilot was Walter Plowden, an ex-slave and Harriet's best agent.

The three ships headed upriver about twenty miles to Field's Point. There, Montgomery stationed some men at an earthworks whose rifle pits had been abandoned by Confederates. The Confederates' flight had been so fast that the blankets they had left behind were still warm. The rest

PLANTATIONS BURN as slaves rush to Union warships that are part of the daring raid Harriet led up the Combahee River.

of Montgomery's men continued up the river, stopping at Tar Bluff, another deserted enemy strongpoint that Harriet's spies had reported.

The remaining men sailed on to Combahee Ferry, where they destroyed a pontoon bridge. Confederate cavalry, caught by surprise, fell back under fire from Montgomery's men and the guns of the *John Adams* and the *Harriet A. Weed*. [5]

Now in military control of the river, Montgomery led the attack on the plantations. He ordered the ships to sound their steam whistles. The blasts echoed across the rice fields. Slaves, startled by the sound, stopped working and looked up to see ships flying the Stars and Stripes. Overseers fled into patches of woods and, waving and firing pistols, ordered the slaves to follow them. Their guns felled some slaves rushing toward the ships.

Black soldiers in rowboats started landing and beckoning. Slaves were running to the warships "from every direction," Harriet later wrote. "I never see such a sight."

One old man later told what had happened when the gunboats came into sight of the slaves who were hoeing in the rice fields. "Then every man drop the hoe, and left the rice." The overseer shouted: "The Yankee come. See you to Cuba! Run for hide!" Everyone started running toward the ships. The overseer was shouting: "Run the other way!" [6]

"We run by him, straight to the boat," the old man remembered. When he got to the ship, he saw black soldiers. "I'm eighty-one years old," the man said. He wondered if he was too old to go off with the black soldiers. Then he decided, "Never too old for leave the land of bondage."

Harriet remembered another scene, at another plantation on the river: "Some was getting their breakfasts, just taking their pots of rice right off the fire, and they'd put a cloth on top their head an set that on, rice a'smoking, young one hanging on behind, one hand round the mother's forehead to hold on, the other hand digging into the rice pot, eating it with all its might....And them that hadn't a pot of rice would have a child in their arms, sometimes one or two

JUBILANT WOMEN, carrying babies, rice pots, and livestock, run to liberators in Union warships.

holding on to their mother's dress." Others were "carrying two children, one astride of the mother's neck, holding on her forehead and another in her arms....I never see so many twins in my life.

"Some had bags on their backs with pigs in them. Some had chickens tied by the legs. And so, child squalling, chickens squawking, and pigs squealing, they all come running to the gunboats through the rice fields just like a procession."

At the riverside, men, women, and children rushed to get into the rowboats. As oarsmen began rowing toward the ships, the next wave of people grabbed the rowboat gunwales to stop them. "The soldiers beat them on the hands," Harriet said. "But they wouldn't let go."

The ship's captain called to her: "Moses, come here and speak a word of consolation to your people!" Harriet didn't like the captain's "your people," thinking "they wasn't my people any more than they was his." But she did sing to them:

Come from the East.
Come from the West...
Come along, come along;
Don't be alarmed,
For Uncle Sam is rich enough
To give you all a farm.

"Then they throwed up their hands and began to rejoice and shout *Glory!* And the rowboats

BLACK SOLDIERS who had been slaves practice their marksmanship before going into battle as part of the Union Army.

would push off. I kept on singing until all were brought on board." [7]

While Harriet managed the passengers clambering aboard the ships, Montgomery was leading the most destructive raid the Lowcountry had ever seen. At one point, a unit of Confederate sharpshooters and cavalrymen appeared and found themselves facing black troops. The ex-slaves, all raw recruits, took a stand, lining up across the road and, firing steadily, held off the Confederates for half an hour. Ship shellfire finally drove back the attackers and the black troops boarded the *John Adams*, which steamed away.

At some stops—apparently places picked by Harriet's spies—slaves waited near the water for the freedom ships. The ships slowly made their way downriver, taking on slaves and dropping off soldiers, who fanned out along the river. The raiders struck at least nine plantations, hardly ever seeing anyone. Some soldiers took away horses or broke into warehouses that spies had reported were full of cotton or rice. As men took the harvests back to the ships, others set out on other missions.

Soldiers set dozens of buildings on fire. And ex-slaves of the rice fields, now wearing Union uniforms, tramped through mud to familiar sluice (sliding) gates set up on dikes along the river. The slaves with the hoes that morning—now fleeing to freedom—had been "hilling up" the young rice plants, getting the tender green shoots just above water. Soon the fields were to be carefully flooded. The sluice gates controlled the flow, skimming the fresh water off the top of the salt water that was brought up the river on the tide. Soldiers now smashed the gates. Water poured into the fields, ruining thousands of acres of what the planters called Carolina gold.

At a horseshoe bend on the Combahee was the Cypress Plantation, owned by Cap'n Bill Heyward. His annual rice crop usually totaled more than one million pounds. On the morning of June 1, a house slave knocked at his door and told him that the slave foreman had spotted three Yankee ships steaming up the river. Heyward grabbed a spyglass and went outside to confirm the report. He called for his horse and rode off to alert the nearest Confederate outpost.

By the time he returned, his plantation was aflame. "They burned every building on the plantation except the negro quarters," he later said—his mansion, his mill, his stables, his river boats, 10,000 bushels of stored rice, and 800 bushels of corn. One hundred and ninety-nine of his slaves had run off.

"Our losses have been frightful," Edward Barnwell Heyward reported. His shocked wife, Tat Heyward, wrote in a letter four days later, "The Yankees have devastated the plantations, six or seven of

SOLDIER STUDENTS pose with their white teachers, Northerners who volunteered to aid ex-slaves, once forbidden to read or write.

them...carrying off six or seven hundred negroes." [8]

Joshua Nicholl watched from the woods as his mansion burned to the ground. He lost a library of 3,500 books and "every material object to which my heart still clung."

Leaving behind the burning plantations, the three ships arrived in Beaufort on the night of June 2. They were brimming over with about 750 freed men, women, children, and babies.* Not a

*The official report says 725; Harriet counted 756.

single soldier had been lost. But, as Harriet put it, "We have good reason to believe that a number of rebels bit the dust."

Proud black Union soldiers, so recently slaves themselves, ushered their passengers into a church in Beaufort, where first Montgomery and then Harriet spoke. We do not have a copy of their words. But a Wisconsin newspaper reporter, who did not know Harriet's name, was awed by "this black heroine," called her Moses, and hailed her for her "patriotism, sagacity, energy, ability, and all that elevates human character."

Hunter was anxious to have Montgomery "repeat his incursions as rapidly as possible in different directions, injuring the enemy all he can and carrying away their slaves, thus rapidly filling up the South Carolina regiments...."

Harriet was determined to go on more "incursions." But, on returning to Beaufort, she was put in charge of the new refugees. She found herself working as a cook and laundry woman to earn extra money to care for the families she was recruiting. One of the people she cooked for was

Colonel Robert Gould Shaw, the white commander of the newly arrived 54th Massachusetts Regiment, a black unit that had been organized in his state by Governor Andrew. Amongst its soldiers were two sons of Frederick Douglass.

Shaw joined Montgomery on a raid that left Darien, Georgia, a smoking ruin. Shaw protested the torching of the town and requested another assignment. When General Quincy A. Gillmore arrived, replacing Hunter, Shaw and the 54th became part of the force that would launch a sea-and-land attack on Charleston. On July 18, Shaw led his men against massive Fort Wagner, which rose above the sands of Morris Island, defending the southern approach to Charleston. Shaw was killed, along with more than a hundred of his men. Charleston did not fall.

Harriet later said she had served Shaw his last breakfast. So she was close enough to hear the attack and feel the battle in her mystical way: "And then we saw the lightning, and that was the guns; and then we heard the thunder, and that was the big guns; and then we heard the rain falling, and that

"MOUND OF FIRE." Soldiers of the all-black 54th Massachusetts Regiment fight their way to Fort Wagner, near Charleston. Of the 600 men who tried to take the fort, nearly 300 fell, dead or wounded, in a day of courage and pride.

was the drops of blood falling, and when we came to get in the crops, it was the dead we reaped." [9]

Harriet was still in Beaufort in February 1864 when an officer from Boston visited her. He found her cooking and washing clothes. But between chores she still spied. "She wants to go North," her visitor wrote in a letter, "but says Gen. Gillmore will not let her go....He thinks her services are too valuable....She has made it a business to see all the contrabands escaping from the rebels, and is able to get more intelligence from them than anybody else."

She did go home for a time. But she was soon back in the war, caring for the wounded at Fortress Monroe, Virginia, a fitting place for her war work to end. For it was at Fortress Monroe where the first contrabands had crossed enemy lines, risking their lives to become spies for the Union.

The war would go on until April 9, 1865, when General Robert E. Lee surrendered his Confederate Army to General Ulysses S. Grant at Appomattox Court House in Virginia. We know what many black spies did for the Union's victory, but we do not know the full story. And we know only part of the great work that Harriet Tubman did as a secret agent.

Black spies worked in the darkness of secrecy and prejudice. Frederick Douglass, although speaking of Harriet Tubman, could have been speaking of all these men and women of the Black Dispatches when he said that only "the midnight sky and the silent stars have been the witness of your devotion to freedom and of your own heroism."

PEACE. A candle on a Bible burns before a picture of Harriet Tubman at her home in Auburn, New York, where she died on March 10, 1913.

Epilogue.

Telling the Secrets.

HOW WE KNOW WHAT WE KNOW ·
DESTROYING THE EVIDENCE · EXAMINING THE
OFFICIAL RECORDS · PROOF OF HARRIET'S SERVICE ·
HARRIET'S DEATH

Good spies know how to keep secrets. Harriet Tubman kept many of her secrets, as did the other African Americans who spied for the Union during the Civil War. To tell the world you were a spy, you have to feel safe. You have to believe that no one will find you and seek revenge. After the war, African Americans who spied did not feel safe enough to reveal their secret lives. And most of them, like Harriet, did not know how to write down their recollections.

The first public information about Harriet as a spy, inspired by newspaper reports of the

Combahee River raid, appeared shortly after it happened. Her old abolitionist friend Franklin B. Sanborn published the story in his anti-slavery newspaper, *The Commonwealth*. In 1869, a few more revelations appeared in *Scenes in the Life of Harriet Tubman*, by Sarah Bradford. More scraps about spying can be found in papers submitted for her during her struggle to get back pay and a soldier's pension.

Documents show that Harriet Tubman was the only woman to lead men into battle in the Civil War. Other documents show that she was paid only $200 (plus the $100 secret service money, which she had to use to support her agents). [1]

Most of the reliable information we have about her spy work comes from a few surviving documents. The only mission for which there are details is the Combahee River raid. But the documents do have references to *expeditions*, not just one expedition. And there are other clues, such as this anecdote from her niece, who, as a young girl, was visiting her aunt. The niece had wandered off from the Auburn house. "Suddenly," she recalled,

"I became aware of something moving toward me in the grass." It was Aunt Harriet (then about eighty-eight years old) showing "the way she had gone by many a sentinel during the war."

Harriet's service in South Carolina in 1863 is well documented. As for what she was doing early in the war, there are some clues. Biographer Sarah Bradford, who talked to Harriet, says she was "sent by Governor Andrew of Massachusetts to the South at the beginning of the War, to act as spy and scout for our armies, and to be employed as hospital nurse when needed." Also, in a letter dictated by Harriet in June 1863, she said, "I have been absent two years almost," an indication that her war service had begun sometime in 1861.

There are not many documents about spying in the Civil War. Spymasters of both North and South got rid of papers after the war to protect their agents. As the Confederate capital of Richmond was about to fall into Union hands in April 1865, intelligence and counterintelligence files were destroyed. After the war, many Union files were given to agents, who could do what they wanted with them.

Many operatives, such as Elizabeth Van Lew, the spymaster in Richmond, destroyed their records. But she did not destroy her diary, perhaps because it was too personally valuable. The diary did produce some clues. (Spies aren't supposed to keep a diary, but they often do.)

Thomas McNiven, one of Elizabeth Van Lew's agents, kept a diary about his work. Although the diary was lost, a descendant quoted McNiven as saying Elizabeth was a great spy.

Very little information is available about another black spy, Mary Jane Richards (also known as Mary Elizabeth Bowser), who was said to have spied as a maid in the home of Confederacy President Jefferson Davis.

Some information about Mary comes from a 20th-century relative. One day, sometime in the 1960s, an elderly cousin asked Mrs. McEva Bowser if she knew anything about her husband's great-great-aunt. She replied that people still didn't talk about her because *she had been a spy.* McEva Bowser said that she had seen a diary containing references to a "Mr. Davis." She said she didn't have any idea who he might be and saw no value to the diary. "So the next time I came across it I just pitched it in the trash can."

Mary Bowser's spying was finally officially acknowledged in 1995, when she was admitted to the U.S. Army Intelligence Hall of Fame.

Military officers wrote thousands of documents that mention intelligence activity. They survive in the 128 volumes of *The War of the Rebellion: A Compilation of the Official Records of the Union and Confederate Armies*, published by the U.S. Government between 1880 and 1900. Some information about Black Dispatches can be found by pouring through these volumes. But many Union intelligence files were separated out of the rest of the official documents—and not found until 1959. [2]

Harriet worked as an agent "within the enemies line," as one document puts it. She died on March 10, 1913, in her home in Auburn, New York. There, she kept the best proof of her service to the Union: her U.S. Army canteen, her haversack—and her musket.

SELECTED BATTLES, Underground Railroad "stations," as well as events and places mentioned in the time line, are shown on this map.

Time Line.

<u>1791</u>
- Slave riot in Haiti frightens American slave owners.

<u>1822</u>
- Probable year of Harriet Tubman's birth in Dorchester County, Maryland.
- Slave revolt fails in South Carolina.

<u>1831</u>
- Nat Turner leads a slave revolt in Virginia. He and 20 other slaves are tried and hanged.

<u>1844</u>
- Harriet marries John Tubman, a free-born black man.
- Jonathan Walker is branded SS (for Slave Stealer) on the hand.

<u>1849</u>
- Harriet escapes and travels the Underground Railroad between Maryland and Pennsylvania.

<u>1850</u>
- Congress passes the Fugitive Slave Act as part of the Compromise of 1850, which admits California to the Union as a free state and ends slave trading (but not slavery) in the District of Columbia.
- Harriet leads her first group of Maryland slaves to freedom

<u>1852</u>
- Harriet Beecher Stowe's *Uncle Tom's Cabin* is published.
- Harriet moves to St. Catharines, in Canada, a safe haven from the Fugitive Slave Act.

<u>1854</u>
- A bloody struggle between slaveholders and abolitionists begins in Kansas.

<u>1855</u>
- John Brown arrives in Kansas to fight for the abolitionists.

<u>1857</u>
- Harriet moves to a home she buys in Auburn, New York.
- Supreme Court, in a case involving ex-slave Dred Scott, rules that slaves are not citizens and so have no rights.

- John Brown meets Harriet;
later, at a secret session in
Canada, he reveals his slave-
liberation plan.

1859

- John Brown leads a raid on the
federal arsenal at Harpers
Ferry. He is tried for treason
against Virginia and hanged in
December.

1860

- Abraham Lincoln is elected
President of the United States.
- Harriet rescues fugitive slave
Charles Nalle in Troy,
New York.
- South Carolina secedes from
the Union, quickly followed
by Mississippi, Florida,
Alabama, Georgia, Louisiana,
and Texas.
- Harriet makes her last trip to
free slaves in Maryland.

1861

- Harriet briefly returns to
Canada as slave catchers look
for her in New York.
- The Confederate States of
America is formed.
- The Civil War begins as
Confederate guns fire on
Fort Sumter.

- Virginia, North Carolina,
Arkansas, and Tennessee join
the Confederacy.
- Pro-slavery mobs in Baltimore
attack Massachusetts soldiers
heading for Washington, D.C.
- Confederates defeat Union
troops at Manassas, Virginia,
in the first major battle of
the Civil War.
- Union warships, carrying out
the Anaconda Plan, blockade
Southern ports.
- Union General Benjamin
F. Butler declares that slaves
fleeing to the Union are
"contraband" of war and
cannot be returned to their
Confederate owners. Ex-slaves
begin spying for Union forces.
- Union officers start calling
intelligence from African
Americans Black Dispatches.
- Harriet becomes a secret agent
for the Union.

1862

- In Richmond, Elizabeth Van
Lew runs a spy ring for the
Union, using both white and
black spies.
- General Grant wins a bloody,
hard-fought battle at Shiloh
in Tennessee.

- Union Navy takes New Orleans.
- Confederates under General Robert E. Lee are defeated at Antietam, Maryland, in the bloodiest battle in U.S. history.
- The battle between two ironclads, the *Virginia* and the *Monitor*, ends the age of wooden warships.
- Robert Smalls, a slave, takes over a Confederate ship in Charleston and presents it to the Union. He and other slaves gain freedom by joining the Union Navy.
- Union land and naval forces invade South Carolina.
- Harriet arrives in South Carolina. She recruits ex-slaves as spies and Union soldiers.
- First Union regiment of black troops is formed.

1863

- The Emancipation Proclamation declares all slaves in Confederate-controlled areas "forever free."
- Harriet directs a raid on the Combahee River and becomes the first woman to lead a U.S. military operation.
- Lee's defeat at the battle of Gettysburg, Pennsylvania, turns the tide of war for the Union.

- The fall of Vicksburg, Mississippi, gives control of the Mississippi River to the Union.

1864

- Union troops capture Atlanta.
- President Lincoln is reelected.
- General Grant attacks Petersburg, just south of Richmond, and begins a nine-month siege.

1865

- Congress approves the Thirteenth Amendment to the United States Constitution, to abolish slavery. The amendment goes to the states for ratification.
- Richmond falls to Union forces.
- General Lee surrenders to General Grant in the village of Appomattox Court House, Virginia, ending the Civil War.
- President Lincoln is assassinated in Washington, D.C., at Ford's Theater.
- Harriet moves back to Auburn, New York.

1870

- Harriet marries Nelson Davis.

1913

- Harriet dies of pneumonia.

Elizabeth
Van Lew's Code.

Elizabeth Van Lew, a Richmond woman who ran a highly successful spy ring for the Union, sent reports in a kind of secret-message system called a "cipher square," in which each letter and number was represented by a two-digit number. She kept the cipher square (recreated and enlarged below)— the key to encrypting her messages—in her watchcase.

6	r	n	b	h	t	x
3	v	I	u	8	4	w
1	e	m	3	j	5	g
5	l	a	9	0	i	d
2	k	7	2	z	6	s
4	p	o	y	c	f	q
	1	3	6	2	5	4

One of her reports, found by historians after the war, was 336 words long. So, on a tiny piece of paper, she had to write about 1,500 letters, substituting two digits for each of those letters.

Members of her ring managed to get all of her messages out of Richmond and into the hands of Union officers outside the Confederate capital. They used their duplicate copy of the cipher square to decipher her messages.

In an encrypted message, the first number tells you which horizontal row to look in; the second number tells you which vertical column to look in. In the cipher square at left, for example, 13 represents the letter m, and 52 represents zero.

Coded messages appear throughout this book. Use Elizabeth Van Lew's code to decipher them, then check your answers on the author's Web site: www.tballen.com.

Text Notes.

PROLOGUE: BLACK MOSES.

[1] In recent years, some people have objected to the word "slave" because, they say, the word is a label that describes a person only as a powerless human being. People who dislike the word "slave" suggest the substitute "enslaved person" because "enslaved" shows that someone else made the person a slave. While respecting the idea that inspired "enslaved person," this book uses "slave," a word whose meaning has been clear since about 1290, when "slave" entered the English language.

CHAPTER 1: HARRIET'S ESCAPE.

[1] It took a long time for Pennsylvania to abolish slavery. In 1780 the state legislature passed the Act for the Gradual Abolition of Slavery, which said that all children of slaves born after 1780 would be free when they became 28 years old. So slavery lingered in Pennsylvania into the next century.

[2] Harriet's exact birthday is unknown because official records were not kept for most people born into slavery.

[3] One tradition has it that the weight was for a scale used in a general store. An old store on Bestpitch Ferry Road in Bucktown, Maryland, may be on the site of the original store.

[4] Medical researchers believe that Harriet Tubman suffered from a form of epilepsy named after parts of the brain called the temporal lobes. Temporal lobe epilepsy (TLE) is sometimes caused by a severe head injury. Here is how one person described TLE: "I get the strangest feeling—most of it can't be put into words. The whole world suddenly seems more real at first. It's as though everything becomes crystal

clear. Then I feel...kind of like being in a dream. It's as if I've lived through this exact moment many times before. I hear what people say, but they don't make sense....The whole thing lasts a minute or two."

[5] Harriet's words come to us indirectly. She could not read or write. So the only way to know exactly what she was thinking is to see what she said to people who wrote down her words. Sarah H. Bradford, one of Harriet's early biographers, talked to her in 1868, when Harriet's memories of the Civil War were fresh. Bradford wrote the words just as she heard them from Harriet's lips—such as *dey* for "they," *dem* for "them," *dese* for "these," and *gwine* for "going." In this book, Harriet's words appear without her dialect.

[6] A safe house does not look different from other nearby houses, but it is really a place prepared to take care of people who are being hunted. Spy agencies like the Central Intelligence Agency keep safe houses so that spies and their handlers can meet without danger.

[7] In 1857, when the U.S. Supreme Court ruled seven to two against the slave Dred Scott, Chief Justice Taney wrote the opinion. Scott, born a slave, had gone to court to get his freedom, pointing out that he had lived in free states. Taney ruled that Scott had no right to go to court because he was not a U.S. citizen and "had no rights which the white man was bound to respect." The Dred Scott decision, hailed by the slave states, outraged abolitionists, inspiring them to defy federal laws about slaves.

CHAPTER 2: THE UNDERGROUND RAILROAD.

[1] Several sources say that Harriet led as many as 300 people to freedom, but modern researchers have shown that the number is closer to seventy. Kate Clifford Larson, author of *Bound for the Promised Land,* has found evidence for about thirteen trips and the conducting of about seventy to eighty people to freedom. Jean M. Humez, author of *Harriet Tubman: The Life and the Life Stories,* believes there were ten or eleven trips and the conducting of fifty-nine to seventy-seven people. No one will ever know how many Maryland slaves were inspired or instructed by Harriet and then left on their own.

[2] Harriet seems like the kind of secret agent described by Peter Earnest, a former Central Intelligence Agency case officer. He believes that some agents are "naturals," who "need virtually no formal training but have an instinct for operations and clandestine work."

[3] Some books about Harriet Tubman put the reward a high as $40,000, but no record shows such a sum. Harriet is the source of the $12,000 reward—an immense sum in those days.

[4] Many Canadians favored the South because they sided with pro-South Great Britain. And some Canadians, who had long feared a U.S. invasion, saw a threat from the North's powerful wartime army if war came.

CHAPTER 3: SLAVE REVOLTS.

[1] The informer was George Wilson, who was against violence. Wilson was later granted his freedom for informing, but he felt so much guilt that he went insane and killed himself.

[2] Because of the illegal voting, Congress did not allow Kansas to become a state until the territorial legislature adopted a new constitution; finally, in 1861, shortly before the start of the Civil War, Kansas was admitted to the Union as a free state.

CHAPTER 4: JOHN BROWN MEETS THE GENERAL.

[1] Ross served as a personal spy in Canada for President Lincoln, who was right in assuming that Confederates would set up spy operations in Canada. Little is known about the work that Ross did for Lincoln. Ross later became a famous naturalist. He collected and classified 570 Canadian bird species; 247 species of mammals, reptiles, and freshwater fish; and 3,400 insect species. He also classified 2,200 species of Canadian flowers and trees.

[2] The Secret Six consisted of Thomas Wentworth Higginson, a Massachusetts minister, a fiery abolitionist, and a friend of the poet Emily Dickinson; Theodore Parker, a minister; Franklin Sanborn, a friend of Ralph Waldo Emerson and Henry David Thoreau, who helped send free-soilers to Kansas; George Luther Stearns, also a leader in the

Kansas emigrant plan; Samuel Gridley Howe, who founded a school for blind people and was the husband of Julia Ward Howe, who wrote "The Battle Hymn of the Republic"; and Gerrit Smith of New York, who gave forty acres in the Adirondacks to poor African Americans so that they would be able to vote as land owners. Smith was also a crusader for women's rights.

[3] For slaves, the Fourth of July had been a day of fear, rather than celebration, ever since 1822 when rumors swept slaves quarters in and around Charleston, South Carolina, that slave owners planned to massacre blacks on July 4. The rumor was one of many said to have inspired the revolt planned by Denmark Vesey. After his plot was revealed, a pamphlet published in Charleston said, "The celebration of the Fourth of July belongs exclusively to the white population of the United States."

[4] Richard Henry Dana, a Boston lawyer and author of *Two Years Before the Mast*, defended Burns in a trial. But the court ruled that he had to be returned to his master. Troops held off a crowd of 50,000 when federal marshals took Burns in chains through the streets of Boston to a federal ship that carried him back to Virginia. Burns was the last slave arrested in New England under the fugitive law. Abolitionists later purchased him to free him. He became the pastor of a church in Canada. Massachusetts later passed futile state laws aimed at preventing the Fugitive Slave Act from being enforced.

CHAPTER 5: TROUBLE AT HARPERS FERRY.

[1] Lee and Stuart would both serve the South during the Civil War: Lee would take command of the Confederate Army, and Stuart would become the Confederacy's most famous cavalry officer.

[2] One of the Virginia militiamen guarding the gallows for fear of a rescue attempt was John Wilkes Booth. He would assassinate President Abraham Lincoln on April 14, 1865.

[3] In time, six other raiders were caught, tried, and hanged. Ten of Brown's men had been killed at Harpers Ferry. Five men escaped,

including Osborne P. Anderson, a printer on the *Provincial Freeman*, a Canadian newspaper edited by Delaware-born Mary Ann Shadd. During the Civil War, Shadd recruited black soldiers for the Union Army. After the war, she attended Howard University Law School and became the first black female lawyer in the United States.

CHAPTER 6: THE "OLD COLORED WOMAN."

[1] The reporter compares Harriet to a Revolutionary War heroine, Mary Hays McCauly (better known as Molly Pitcher), who carried water in a pitcher to her husband and his gun crew during the battle of Monmouth (New Jersey) on June 28, 1778. When her husband was wounded, she replaced him at the cannon.

CHAPTER 7: TROUBLE IN THE CAPITAL.

[1] The Border States, which shared their borders with states of the Confederacy, were Delaware, Maryland, Kentucky, and Missouri. These states teetered between North and South while staying in the Union. After Virginia's western counties pulled out of the state and became West Virginia in 1863, the new state became a Border State.

[2] At that time, the President was inaugurated on March 4. Winter travel was so difficult that it was necessary to have a long period between the November election and the inauguration. The Twentieth Amendment to the Constitution, ratified in 1933, changed the date to January 20.

CHAPTER 8: THE SECRET WAR.

[1] During the war, neither the North nor the South had an organized intelligence service. But both sides used the words "secret service" to describe activities that included using spies, breaking codes, and sending out counterspies to track down spies and sabotage missions.

[2] Virginia, Arkansas, North Carolina, and Tennessee refused and seceded. Virginia troops seized Federal arsenals at Norfolk and Harpers Ferry. Union soldiers crossed the Potomac River to Virginia, taking Alexandria and Arlington Heights to protect Washington. Both sides

eventually realized they could not rely only on volunteers. The Union began drafting men in the summer of 1863, less than a year after the Confederacy passed its own draft act. In both the North and the South, men could legally avoid being drafted by hiring substitutes.

[3] Southerners nicknamed Butler "the Beast" for his harsh command of Union-controlled New Orleans later in the war.

[4] A fortress is more than a fort; it is a fortified enclosure, covering a large area. Monroe's 35-foot walls enclosed about 70 acres.

CHAPTER 9: BLACK DISPATCHES.

[1] The Union prisoners were sent to Andersonville, Georgia, where the Confederates had one of the most horrible prison camps of the war. The Andersonville prison lasted for 15 months. During that time, nearly 13,000 Union prisoners died there of starvation and disease.

[2] Liberia, on Africa's west coast, was founded in 1822 by "free men of color" under the sponsorship of the American Colonization Society. The migration of American blacks to Liberia was supported by many white Americans, including President Lincoln and Harriet Beecher Stowe.

[3] In 1905, Varina Davis, Jefferson Davis's widow, denied that a Union spy had worked in the mansion. "My maid," she wrote, "was an ignorant girl brought up on our plantation who would not have done anything to injure her master or me." She did not mention her coachman or the slaves who tried to burn down the Richmond White House. More information on Mary Bowser came in the 1960s (see pages 166–167).

CHAPTER 10: BLACK SPIES AND THE ANACONDA PLAN.

[1] African American slaves could be set free by their masters or their masters' heirs. Or a slave could work to earn enough money to buy freedom, paying the price paid in the slave market. A Virginia law passed in 1806 forced freed slaves to leave the state within a year after "manumission," the act of releasing a person from slavery. Later changes in the law allowed Virginians to get special permission from the state legislature for ex-slaves to be allowed to live free in the state. Mary

Touvestre (sometimes spelled Louvestre) apparently had such freedom.

[2] The *Virginia* and the *Monitor* dueled off Hampton Roads, Virginia, on March 8, 1862. In this first battle ever fought between ironclads, the ships sometimes were only ten yards apart. Shells bounced off each ship's clanging iron side. The duel ended in a draw. The *Virginia* survived only until May when her crew destroyed her as the Confederates abandoned Norfolk. The *Monitor* sank on December 30, 1862, during a storm off Cape Hatteras, North Carolina.

[3] The Civil War is often called a war in which brother fought brother. This really happened during the Battle of Port Royal. Thomas Drayton commanded Confederate forces and his brother Percival commanded a Union warship that fired on Thomas Drayton's fort. Both brothers survived.

[4] "For some men like 18- and 19-year-old Gabriel and Plenty Seneca, enlistment gave them not only a new social status but also transformed how they identified themselves," writes historian Lisa Y. King. They had enlisted on board the U.S.S. *Seneca* "and took as their surname the name of the ship upon which they had been reborn as free men."

[5] After the war, Elizabeth Van Lew, who ran a Union spy network in Richmond, displayed a photograph of Andrew in her parlor. There is a strong hint that they had known each other during the secret war of spies. In a letter written in 1866, Andrew says that she is "one of the most devoted, hearty, intelligent friends of the Union...I ever knew."

CHAPTER 11: HARRIET GOES TO WAR.

[1] Uncle Remus speaks Gullah in Joel Chandler Harris's Bre'r Rabbit tales.

[2] The earliest records of Harriet's wartime work indicate that she gathered intelligence in Maryland and Virginia. She was almost certainly given missions by Governor Andrew, Secretary of State Seward, and Secretary of War Edwin M. Stanton. On January 7, 1863, a record shows, she was given $100 in "secret service money." What she did with that money is not recorded. To buy today what $100 would buy in 1861, you would need more than $2,000.

[3] To find out what happened when a modern chemist found a buried vial for a torpedo, see http://www.sc.edu/library/socar/uscs/98spsr/wateree.html.

CHAPTER 12: THE GENERAL LEADS A RAID.

[1] In December 1863, Smalls was piloting the *Planter* off Folly Island, near Charleston, when she came under fire. The captain fled from the pilot house and hid in a coal bunker. Smalls took over the ship and brought her safely to port. He was promoted to captain and commanded the *Planter* for the rest of the war.

[2] On May 22, 1863, most units of black troops—under white officers—were segregated in the U.S. Army as "the United States Colored Troops." But black units in Massachusetts and Connecticut, such as the 54th Massachusetts Infantry Regiment, kept their state names throughout the war. By the end of the war, there were about 179,000 black men in the Union Army and 19,000 in the Navy. African Americans would continue to be segregated until President Harry S. Truman officially desegregated the U.S. armed forces in 1948. Truman's order was mostly ignored until President Dwight D. Eisenhower ordered its enforcement in 1953.

[3] Kansas lore traces "jayhawk" to an Irish settler who came back from a looting expedition against slaveholders. He said that an Irish bird called the jayhawk attacked other birds with the delight of a cat attacking a mouse.

[4] Much of the old course of the Combahee River was wiped out in the 1940s, when Lake Marion was created, covering about 110,000 acres of land in five South Carolina counties.

[5] Near the ferry stop, archaeologists have found a cemetery where two black soldiers of the raid regiment were buried, probably after the war. Also found were bits of scorched glass, perhaps relics of the raid.

[6] When the overseer said, "See you to Cuba!" he was spreading a piece of Confederate propaganda. Slaves throughout the South were being warned by their masters that Union soldiers sent runaways to Cuba, where they were sold to work on sugar plantations. Cuba did not outlaw slavery until 1888.

[7] After the raid, Harriet wrote to friends in Boston asking that she be sent "bloomers," a woman's garment consisting of loose, baggy pants gathered at the ankles, under a skirt ending at mid-calf. In an era of hoopskirts and layers of petticoats, bloomers were shocking and denounced as immoral. Bloomers were named after Amelia Jenks Bloomer, an activist in the early women's rights movement. Harriet's request shows her knowledge of a garment that symbolized the movement. After the war, Harriet became a frequent speaker at meetings about women's rights.

[8] Tat Heyward's sister Elizabeth was married to Major Robert Anderson, the Union officer who had surrendered Fort Sumter in April 1861.

[9] Harriet saw the dead and dying of the 54th Massachusetts Regiment at the hospital for black soldiers. One of the white nurses at the white hospital was Clara Barton, who would found the American Red Cross. There is no record that they ever met.

EPILOGUE: TELLING THE SECRETS.

[1] Although Harriet's war service is documented, she never received a military pension for serving in the Union Army. As the widow of Nelson Davis, a black soldier she had met in South Carolina and married in 1869 (her first husband, John Tubman, had been murdered by a white man in 1867), she received a widow's pension of $8 a month, beginning in 1890. On January 19, 1899, this amount was officially increased to $25 a month. However, Harriet never received more than $20 per month until her death on March 10, 1913. In 2003, at the urging of Senator Hillary Rodham Clinton, Congress authorized a payment of $11,750 for the Harriet Tubman Home in Auburn, New York. The amount represents the additional $5 she should have received each month between January 1899 and March 1913, adjusted for interest and the changing value of the dollar.

[2] The files—"a half-roomful" of them—were found at the National Archives by Edwin C. Fishel, a former intelligence officer at the top-secret National Security Agency. He used the files to write *The Secret War for the Union* (see Further Reading, page 187).

Appendix IV.

Quote Sources.

Note: Full bibliographic information is listed only after the first reference or for sources not listed in Further Reading on pages 187–188. If an author has written more than one book, the title referred to is in parentheses. The notation *"OR"* means *"Official Records"* and refers to the 128-volume *The War of the Rebellion: A Compilation of the Official Records of the Union and Confederate Armies*. Washington, D.C.: Government Printing Office; 1880–1900. They can be searched online at several sites, including: http://cdl.library.cornell.edu/moa/browse.monographs/waro.html and http://ehistory.osu.edu/uscw/Library/org.

PROLOGUE: BLACK MOSES.
p. 10 "When...Promised Land." Humez, p. 215; p. 13 Douglass quote is from Rose.

CHAPTER 1: HARRIET'S ESCAPE.
p. 19 "with the blood...couldn't see." Larson, p. 42; p. 20 "I could...shoulder." Dorchester County (MD) Inventory of African American Historical and Cultural Resources; p. 23 "There...strength lasted." Bradford *(Moses of Her People)* p. 29; pp. 23–24 "We fed...go with them." Larson, p. 81; p. 25 "Thou has...befriend him." http://www.russpickett.com/history/garrbio.htm; "I looked...heaven." Bradford *(Moses)*, p. 30.

CHAPTER 2: THE UNDERGROUND RAILROAD.
p. 29 "branded palm...the slave." From "The Branded Hand," by John Greenleaf Whittier; p. 31 "Yes,...coward man?" *Commonwealth* (Boston), July 17, 1863; p. 33 "every slaveholder...live." William Lloyd Garrison, http://www.hfac.uh.edu/gl/abol3.htm; p. 34 "heard...stories" and "the

indelible...their bodies." *Memoirs of a Reformer,* by Alexander Milton Ross. Toronto: Hunter, Rose and Company, 1893.

CHAPTER 3: SLAVE REVOLTS.

p. 41 "I advise...revolver." *A Standard History of Kansas and Kansans,* written and compiled by William E. Connelley, Secretary of the Kansas State Historical Society. Chicago: Lewis Publishing Co., 1918. Online at http://skyways.lib.ks.us/genweb/archives/1918ks/biom/montgoj.html.

CHAPTER 4: BROWN MEETS THE GENERAL.

pp. 47-48 "I was...speak to me." Humez, p. 124; p. 49 "his brave...courageous spirit." Bradford *(Moses)*, p. 96; "could command...right quality." Larson, pp. 159, 160; p. 51 "What...a sham." Douglass, July 5, 1852, Rochester, NY. See http://douglassarchives.org/doug_a10.htm; pp. 51-52 "one...this continent." Humez, p. 35; p. 52 "a conductor...Railroad." *The Unitarians and the Universalists,* by David Robinson. Westport, CT: Greenwood Press, 1985; p. 53 "Come with me...hive them." Allen, p. 33; p. 54 "I believe...old man." http://www.iath.virginia.edu/jbrown/fdlife.html.

CHAPTER 5: TROUBLE AT HARPERS FERRY.

p. 61 "Never mind...fire!" *R. E. Lee: A Biography,* by Douglas Southall Freeman. New York: Charles Scribner's Sons, 1934. Chapter 23; p. 62 "is desirous...may be." *Recollections of Seventy Years,* by F. B. Sanborn, Boston: Gorham Press, 1909. Vol. 1, p. 167 (letter from Sanborn to Higginson, June 4, 1859); pp. 62-63 "I deny...the slaves." http://www.nationalcenter.org/.

CHAPTER 6: THE "OLD COLORED WOMAN."

p. 68 "the favors...brethren." http://www.civilwar.si.edu/slavery_ruffin.html ; pp. 68-69 "who,...numbered." http://www.digitalhistory.uh.edu/database/article_display.cfm?HHID=337; p. 69 "secret emissaries...insurrection." Allen, p. 41; "Then and...blood shed." "Recollections of the John Brown Raid by a Virginian Who Witnessed the Fight," by Alexander Boteler. *Century Magazine,* July 1883, pp. 399-411; p. 71 "an old...woman," *Troy* (NY) *Whig,* April 28, 1859.

CHAPTER 7: TROUBLE IN THE CAPITAL.

p. 78 "There is now...months,"and "Civil War,...the sun." *Civil War Chronicle*, edited by J. Matthew Gallman. New York: Crown Publishers, 2000, p. 23; p. 81 "I have...it exists." Allen, p. 50.

CHAPTER 8: THE SECRET WAR.

p. 83 "from...fund" *Collected Works of Abraham Lincoln*, Vol. 4; letter to William H. Seward, April 2, 1861; p. 91 "George Scott...pistol." *OR*, Series 1, Vol. 2, p. 83; p. 93 "Virginia...country." and "contrabands of war" Guernsey, p. 201.

CHAPTER 9: BLACK DISPATCHES.

p. 96 "If I...I want." Markle, p. 62; p. 97 "of the...courageous" and "kept...guides" and "invaluable...indispensable" and p. 98 "bringing us...ascertained." From "Report of the Services Rendered By the Freed People to the United States Army," by Vincent Colyer. Online at http://www.rootsweb.com/~ncusct/freemen.htm; "second Underground Railroad" http://www.umuc.edu/fyionline/may_03/fyionline7.html; p. 104 "from...Richmond" http://www.cia.gov/cia/publications/civilwar/docs/p11.htm; p. 105 "disbanded...horses" and "It is...prisoners." *OR*, Series 1, Vol. 33, pp. 519–521; p. 106 "greater portion...1864–65" Markle, p. 180; p. 109 "colored girl...best" and "had...mind." and "Everything...information." "Recollections of Thomas McNiven...," archives of Museum of the Confederacy, Richmond; p. 110 "He reports...Richmond." *OR*, Series 1, Vol. 51 (Part 1), p. 597 and Series 1, Vol. 12 (Part III), p. 131; p. 111 "Who comes?...Light and Loyalty." Markle, p. 62; "The chief...Negroes." Rose, http://www.cia.gov/csi/books/dispatches/dispatch.html.

CHAPTER 10: BLACK SPIES AND THE ANACONDA PLAN.

p. 116 "the ship...armament." "The First Iron-Clad Monitor," by Secretary of the Navy Gideon Welles in *The Annals of the War*, available at http://www.civilwarhome.com/monitor.htm; p. 117 "the *Virginia*...supplies." Rose; p. 119 "Good...sir!" *Heroes in Black Skins*, by Booker T. Washington. University of Virginia Library, Chapter 4. Online at http://etext.virginia.

edu/toc/modeng/public/WasHero.html and at http://www.africawithin. com/bios/robert_smalls.htm; "The noise...one time." "Port Royal Expedition, Nov. 1861" by Max Shaw http://www.awod.com/cwchas/ portry.html; p. 121 "came flocking...gunny-sacks." "Indian and Freedman Occupation at the Fish Haul Site, Beaufort County, South Carolina." Michael B. Trinkley, editor, Chicora Foundation Research Series 7, Columbia, SC.; "carrying...be free." Guelzo, p. 72; p. 125 "Once let... citizenship." McPherson *(The Negro's Civil War)* p. 163; "Harriet...scouts." Humez, pp. 51-52.

CHAPTER 11: HARRIET GOES TO WAR.

p. 127 "the most...America," *The History of Beaufort County, South Carolina,* Volume 1, 1514-1861, by Lawrence S. Rowland, Alexander Moore, and George C. Rogers, Jr., Columbia, SC: University of South Carolina Press, 1996, pp. 375-381; p. 128 "If you...leisure." Heyward Family Papers, 1790-1893, Manuscripts Division, Caroliniana Library, Columbia, SC; p. 129 "They were...ditches..." *Fifty Years In Chains, or The Life of an American Slave,* by Charles Ball, Electronic Edition, University of North Carolina at Chapel Hill, http://ibiblio.lsu.edu/main/ Docsouth/ball/ball.xml; pp. 131-132 "They laughed...no how" and "every-thing...sing" and "a great...at all." Bradford *(Moses),* p. 103; p. 132 Gullah quotes: "Living Soul of Gullah" by John H. Tibbetts. *Coastal Heritage,* Volume 14, Number 4, Spring 2000, and "The Gullah Dialect and Sea Island Culture," Part I, "The Gullah Dialect," by Dennis Adams and Hillary Barnwell. Beaufort County Public Library. See http://www. bcgov.net/bftlib/gullah.htm; p. 135 "dying...sheep" and "dug...cured them." Bradford *(Scenes in the Life of Harriet Tubman),* pp. 37-38.

CHAPTER 12: THE GENERAL LEADS A RAID.

p. 140 "I always...so its is." and p. 141 "Governor...hands." *The Complete Civil War Journal and Selected Letters of Thomas Wentworth Higginson,* edited by Christopher Looby. University of Chicago Press, 1999 ("Camp Saxon, Feb. 4, 1862"); p. 143 "much...information." and "Never...up!" *Army*

Life in a Black Regiment, by Thomas Wentworth Higginson. Fields, Osgood, 1870, Chapter 3; p. 144 "No officer...black ones...." "Report of Col. T. W. Higginson," February 1, 1863, *OR*, Series I, Vol. 14, pp. 195-198; p. 145 "are outlawed...God." *Blue-Eyed Child of Fortune: The Civil War Letters of Colonel Robert Gould Shaw*, edited by Russell Duncan, University of Georgia Press, 1992, pp. 341-345; p. 149 "When we...to the field." and p. 151 "from every...sight." Humez, p. 241 (from account written by Emma Paddock Telford); "Then every...bondage!" *Historical Atlas of the Rice Plantations of the ACE River Basin–1860*, by Suzanne Cameron Linder. South Carolina Department of Archives & History, 1995, pp. 131-32; pp. 152-154 "Some was...procession." and "The soldiers...let go." and Harriet's song and "Moses,...your people!" Humez, pp. 245-246 (from Telford account); pp. 156-157 "They burned...quarters." and "Our losses... negroes." Heyward Family Papers, 1790-1893; "every...still clung." *Historical Atlas of the Rice Plantations of the ACE River Basin–1860*, p 514; p. 158 "We have...the dust." *Commonwealth* (Boston), July 10 1863, as quoted in Larson, p. 216; "this black heroine" and "patriotism...character." *Wisconsin State Journal* (Madison), June 20, 1863, as quoted in Larson, p. 214; "repeat...regiments..." *OR*, Series 1, Vol. 14 (part 1), p. 463; pp. 159-160 "And then...we reaped" *Famous Negro Heroes of America*, by Langston Hughes. New York: Dodd Mead, 1958, p. 263; pp. 160-161 "She wants... anybody else." Larson, p. 222; p. 161 "the midnight...heroism." Frederick Douglass letter to Harriet Tubman, August 29, 1868.

EPILOGUE: TELLING THE SECRETS.
pp. 164-65 "Suddenly,...war." Larson, p. 288, quoting from a recollection given to Earl Conrad, who wrote an early biography; "sent by...needed" Bradford *(Moses)*, p. 6; and "I have...1861." Bradford *(Moses)* p. 84; pp. 166-67 "Mr. Davis...trash can." Report by Vertamae Grosvenor on National Public Radio's "Morning Edition," April 19, 2002.

Appendix V.

Further Reading.

Allen, Thomas B. *The Blue and the Gray.* Washington, DC: National Geographic Society, 1992.

Bradford, Sarah H. *Scenes in the Life of Harriet Tubman.* Auburn, NY: W. J. Moses, 1869. Online at http://docsouth.unc.edu/neh/bradford/menu.html.

_____. *Harriet: The Moses of Her People.* New York: G. R. Lockwood & Son, 1886. Online at http://docsouth.unc.edu/harriet/harriet.htm.

Clinton, Catherine. *Harriet Tubman: The Road to Freedom.* New York: Little, Brown, and Company 2004.

Conrad, Earl. *Harriet Tubman.* Washington, DC: The Associated Publishers, 1943.

Fishel, Edwin C. *The Secret War for the Union.* Boston: Houghton Mifflin, 1996.

Guernsey, Alfred H. and Henry M. Alden. *Harper's Pictorial History of The Civil War.* New York: Fairfax Press, 1886.

Guelzo, Allen C. *Lincoln's Emancipation Proclamation.* New York: Simon & Schuster, 2004.

Higginson, Thomas Wentworth. *Army Life in a Black Regiment.* Boston: Fields, Osgood & Co., 1870.

_____. *The Complete Civil War Journal and Selected Letters of Thomas Wentworth Higginson.* Christopher Looby, editor. University of Chicago Press, 1999.

Humez, Jean M. *Harriet Tubman: The Life and the Life Stories.* Madison: University of Wisconsin Press, 2003.

Larson, Kate Clifford. *Bound for the Promised Land: Harriet Tubman: Portrait of an American Hero.* New York: Ballantine Books, 2004.

Markle, Donald E. *Spies and Spymasters of the Civil War.* New York: Hippocrene Books, 2004.

McPherson, James M. *Battle Cry of Freedom.* New York: Oxford University Press, 1988.

_____. *The Negro's Civil War.* New York: Vintage Books, 1991.

Quarles, Benjamin. *The Negro in the Civil War.* Boston: Little, Brown and Company, 1953.

Rose, P. K. "The Civil War: Black American Contributions to Union Intelligence." *Studies in Intelligence.* Winter 1998–1999, published by the Central Intelligence Agency's Center for the Study of Intelligence. Online at http://www.cia.gov/csi/books/dispatches/dispatch.html.

Tidwell, William A., with James O. Hall and David Winfred Gaddy. *Come Retribution.* Jackson: University Press of Mississippi, 1988.

Van Lew, Elizabeth L. *A Yankee Spy in Richmond: The Civil War Diary of "Crazy Bet" Van Lew.* Davis D. Ryan, editor. Harrisburg, PA: Stackpole, 1996.

Varon, Elizabeth R. *Southern Lady, Yankee Spy.* New York: Oxford University Press, 2003.

The Index.

Italic indicates illustrations.

A

Abolitionists 29, 32–35, 39–40, *41*, 43, 66, 75, 87
Anaconda Plan 113–114, 117, 119
    map 114
Anderson, Robert 80–81
Andrew, John A. 6, *6*, 93
    abolitionism 123–124, 125, 141
    Civil War role 87, 88, 90, 137, 141, 159, 165

B

Beaufort, South Carolina 127–128, 131–133, 142, 157–158, 160
Beecher, Henry Ward 40–41
Bowser, Mary Elizabeth 7, *7*, 106–110, *109*, 166–167
Bowser, McEva 166–167
Bowser, Wilson 108
Bradford, Sarah H. 71, 164, 165
Brisby, William 102
Brown, Henry *26*
Brown, John 6, *6*, *44*
    Harpers Ferry raid *52*–*65*, 69, 75
    and Harriet Tubman 46–50, 51–52
    Kansas raids 42–43, 51
    slave revolt plans 43–51, *68*, 137
Buchanan, James 57
Burns, Anthony 6, *6*, 52, *53*
Butler, Benjamin F. 7, *7*, 87, 89–93, *92*, 95, 103, 104

C

Charleston, South Carolina 80, *85*, 85–86, 118–119, 121, *123*, 158–159, *160*

Codes 98–100, 103, *103*, 172
Combahee River, South Carolina 145–156, *150*, 163–164
Confederate States of America 80
    map 14–15, 168
Contrabands 7, *7*, *92*, 93, 95

D

Davis, Jefferson
    servants 106–110, *109*, 166–167
Dixon, Jeremiah 17–18
Douglass, Frederick 6, *6*, 34, *47*, 159
    and John Brown 46, 50, 53–54
    writings 13, 51, 125, 161
Dupont, Samuel F. 119, 121–122

E

Edmonds, Sarah Emma 96
Emancipation Proclamation 137, 141, *141*

F

Fort Sumter, Charleston, South Carolina 80, *82*, *85*, 86
Fortress Monroe, Virginia 90–93, *92*, *94*, 95, 161
Frémont, John C. 125
Fugitive Slave Act 30, 33, 66, 92

G

Garrett, Thomas 24–25
Garrison, William Lloyd 39–40
Gillmore, Quincy A. 159, 160
Grant, Ulysses S. 105, 161
Green, Shields 54, 61
Green, Harriet 18

H

Haiti, West Indies
    slave revolt *36*, 37–38, 64

Harpers Ferry, Virginia
   John Brown's raid 52, *56–61*, 69
Hawkins, Rush 96
Heyward family 128, 147–148, 156
Hicks, Thomas 77–78, 79
Higginson, Thomas 6, *6, 53,* 93
   Civil War 136–137, 139–144, *142*
   and John Brown 52, 62, 63–64
Hunter, David 7, *7,* 123–125, 136,
   143–145, 158–159

J

Jackson, William A. 109–110
John Adams (ship) 140, 149, 150,
   155

K

Kansas Territory 40–43

L

Lee, Robert E. 57, 59–61, 111, 161
Lincoln, Abraham
   call for volunteers 86, 87
   Emancipation Proclamation 137
   Inaugural Address *76,* 81
   opponents 78, *79*
   preserving Union 14, 81, 124
   and slavery 14, 78, 81, 124–125
   spy network 46, 81, 83–84

M

Maryland
   as Border State 17–18, 87
   slavery 18, 77–78, 79
   Southern sympathizers 88–90,
      89
Mason, Charles 17–18
Mason-Dixon Line 17–18
Massachusetts troops 87, 88–90,
   89, 159–160, *160*
McDowell, Irvin 109–110
McNiven, Thomas 108–109, 166
Monitor, U.S.S. (gunboat) 116, *117*
Montgomery, James 6, *6*

Civil War raids 144–145, 146,
   148–150, 154, 158
   and John Brown 63–64, 136, 137

N

Nalle, Charles 71–74
New York troops *86,* 90
Nicholl, Joshua 157
Norfolk, Virginia 114–115, 117

P

Planter (ship) 118–119, 140
Plowden, Walter 149
Port Royal Island, South Carolina
   119–121

Q

Quakers 23–25

R

Richmond, Virginia
   spies 100–107
Ross, Alexander 6, *6,* 34–35, 46
Ross, Benjamin 18
Ruffin, Edmund 67–68

S

Sanborn, Franklin B. 164
Savannah, Georgia *79,* 122–123
Scobell, John 7, *7,* 110–111
Scott, Dred 84–85
Scott, George 90–91
Scott, Winfield 114
Secession 67, 68–69, 78, 80
Secret Six 6, 46, 61–62, 70, 80
Seward, William H. 7, *7,* 83–84, 93
Sharpe, George H. 105–106
Shaw, Robert Gould 159
Slaves
   catchers *33,* 66, 77, 78, 80
   contrabands 7, *7, 92,* 93, 95
   freed by Union troops *120,* 121,
      123, *150,* 150–154, *152*
   laws about 29–30, 40, 41, 84–85
   plantation life 10, *128–131*

punishment *19*, 129, 143
revolt plans 43, 45–55, 57–59,
        64–65, 68–69, 77–78, 79,
        137
revolts *36*, 37–40, 64
runaways *16*, 28–29, *33*, 91, *92*, 93,
        95–98, 136
sale of 20–21, *21*
as spies 10, 91, 93, 95–98, 97, *99*
Smalls, Robert 7, *7*, 117–119, 122, 140
Smith, Gerrit 70–71, 80, 93
South Carolina
    map of coastline 147
    secession 78, 80
    slavery 38, 123, 128–131, 146, 147,
        150, 151–156
Spying
    codes 98–100, *99*, 103, *103*, 172
    procedures 31–32, 35, 70, 84, 97,
        102, 103–104, *104*
Stanton, Edwin M. 104, 110
Stuart, J. E. B. "Jeb" 57, 59–61

T

Taney, Roger B. 24–25
Todd, David H. 101–102
Torpedo mines *123*, *126*, 133–134, *134*,
        135, 145–146
Touvestre, Mary 115 117
Tubman, Harriet 6, *6*, *162*
    childhood 18–20
    Civil War role 87, 145–158, 164,
        165, 167
    escape from slavery 9–11, 21–24
    family 20–21, 84, 164–165
    freeing Charles Nalle 69–75, *72*
    friendship with Seward 83, 84, 93
    head injury 18–19
    jobs 134–135, 158–159
    and John Brown 46–50, 51–52, 58,
        61, 62, 64

marriage 20, 30
name 18, 20
nicknames 8, 11, 12, 18, 49
recruitment of ex-slaves 131–133,
        134, 136, 144
and slave catchers *22*, 32, 80
slave life 9–10
spying *2*, 12–13, 87, 125, 163–165
and Underground Railroad *8*, 11,
        25, 30–31, 33–34, 77,
        78–79
visions 19–20, 47–49, *48*, 58
Tubman, John 20, 21–22, 30
Turner, Nat 38–40, *39*, 68

U

Underground Railroad *16*, 27–28,
        33, 33–34, 35, 78
Union forces *135*
    assistance from slaves 98–100
    black troops 122, 124–125, 133,
        136, *137*, 139–144, *142*, *154*,
        154–155, *157*, 158–159
    military structure 87–88
    naval blockade *112*, 113–114
    spies 13, 95–111, 115–119, 121–122,
        165–167
    woman soldier 96
United States
    map 14–15, 168

V

Van Lew, Elizabeth 7, *7*, 100–107, *101*,
        104, 166, 172
Vesey, Denmark 38
Virginia, C.S.S. (ship) 115–117, *117*
Virginia slave revolts 38–40

W

Walker, Jonathan 28–29
Washington, Lewis 58, 61
Welles, Gideon 116, 122, 124
Whittier, John Greenleaf 29

CREDITS.

KEY— BE: Bettmann; CEP: from "The Civil War at Charleston," *The News and Courier, Charleston Evening Post*; CB: Carla Bauer; CO: Corbis; CW: Civilwarphotos.net; GC: The Granger Collection, New York; LOC: Library of Congress; NGIC: National Geographic Image Collection; NWPA: North Wind Picture Archive; NYPL: New York Public Library; OHS: Ohio Historical Society; SC: Schomburg Center for Research in Black Culture.

1 (top): © Vladimir Kordic; 1 (bottom): SC; 2: © Paul Collins/Collins Art; 6 (r-l, t-b): OHS; BE/CO; OHS; OHS; Boston Public Library; LOC; Kansas State Historical Society; NYPL; 7 (r-l, t-b): LOC; LOC; Virginia Historical Society; CW; LOC; LOC; CW; 8: © Jerry Pinkney/NGIC; 16: GC; 19: LOC; 21: Chicago Historical Society; 22: Delaware Historical Society; 26: Friends Historical Society of Swarthmore College; 29: Private Collection; 33: NWPA; 36: GC; 39: GC; 41: CB; 42: NWPA; 44: Painting by Ole Peter Hansen Balling, National Portrait Gallery, Smithsonian Institution/Art Resource; 47: GC; 48: CB; 53: GC; 54: CB; 56: SC/NYPL; 59: NYPL; 60: BE/CO; 63: SC/NYPL; 66: LOC; 68: CB; 72: CB; 76: LOC; 79: LOC; 82: Painting by Conrad Wise Chapman, BE/CO; 85: NWPA; 86: The Seventh Regiment Fund/NGIC; 89: NYPL; 92: Fort Monroe Museum; 94: LOC; 99: CB; 101: CO; 103: Museum of the Confederacy; 104: CB; 109: CB; 112: NYPL; 114: LOC; 117: CO; 120: GC; 123: CEP; 126: LOC; 129: The Georgia Archives; 130: LOC; 134: CO; 135: CEP; 138: FDR Library, NY; 141: LOC; 142: CB; 150: CEP; 152: CB; 154: LOC; 157: LOC; 160: GC; 162: © Louie Psihoyos/CO.

ABOUT THE NATIONAL GEOGRAPHIC SOCIETY.

One of the world's largest nonprofit scientific and educational organizations, the National Geographic Society was founded in 1888 "for the increase and diffusion of geographic knowledge." Fulfilling this mission, the Society educates and inspires millions every day through its magazines, books, television programs, videos, maps and atlases, research grants, the National Geographic Bee, teacher workshops, and innovative classroom materials. The Society is supported through membership dues, charitable gifts, and income from the sale of its educational products. This support is vital to National Geographic's mission to increase global understanding and promote conservation of our planet through exploration, research, and education.

For more information, please call 1-800-NGS LINE (647-5463)
or write to the following address:

NATIONAL GEOGRAPHIC SOCIETY
1145 17th Street N.W.
Washington, D.C. 20036-4688 U.S.A.
Visit the Society's Web site at www.nationalgeographic.com.